# LEARNING ADVENTURES:
# SPORTS
## Grades 5–6

By the Staff of Score@Kaplan

Foreword by Alan Tripp

Simon & Schuster

**This series is dedicated to our
Score@Kaplan parents and children—
thank you for making these books possible.**

Published by
Kaplan Educational Centers and Simon & Schuster
1230 Avenue of the Americas
New York, NY 10020

Special thanks to: Elissa Grayer, Doreen Beauregard, Julie Schmidt, Rebecca Geller
Schwartz, Linda Lott, Janet Cassidy, Marlene Greil, Nancy McDonald, Sarah Jane
Bryan, Chris Wilsdon, Janet Montal, Jeannette Sanderson, David Stienecker, Dan
Greenberg, Kathy Wilmore, Dorrie Berkowitz, Brent Gallenberger, and Molly Walsh

Head Coach and General Manager, Score@Kaplan: Alan Tripp
President, Score@Kaplan: Robert L. Waldron
Series Content and Development: Mega-Books
Project Editor: Mary Pearce
Production Editor: Donna Mackay, Graphic Circle Inc.
Art Director: Elana Goren-Totino
Illustrators: Rick Brown, Ryan Brown, Jim Ceribello, Sandy Forrest, Larry Nolte,
Evan Polenghi, Fred Schrier, Peter Spacek, Arnie Ten
Cover Design: Cheung Tai
Cover Photograph: Michael Britto

Manufactured in the United States of America
Published Simultaneously in Canada

January 1998
10 9 8 7 6 5 4 3 2 1

ISBN:0-684-84438-9

# Contents

# Dear Parents,

Your child's success in school is important to you, and at Score@Kaplan we are always pleased when the kids who attend our educational centers do well on their report cards. But what we really want for our kids is not just good grades. We also want everything that good grades are supposed to represent:

- We want our kids to master the key communication systems that make civilization possible: language (spoken and written), math, the visual arts, and music.
- We want them to build their critical-thinking skills so they can understand, appreciate, and improve their world.
- We want them to continually increase their knowledge and to value learning as the key to a happy, successful life.
- We want them to always do their best, to persist when challenged, to be a force for good, and to help others whenever they can.

These are ambitious goals, but our children deserve no less. We at Score@Kaplan have already helped thousands of children across the country in our centers, and we hope this series of books for children in first through sixth grades will reach many more households.

## Simple Principles

We owe the remarkable success of Score@Kaplan to a few simple principles. This book was developed with these principles in mind.

- We expect every child to succeed.
- We make it possible for every child to succeed.
- We reinforce every instance of success, no matter how small.

## Assessing Your Child

One helpful approach in assessing your child's skills is to ask yourself the following questions.

- How much is my child reading? At what level of difficulty?
- Has my child mastered appropriate language arts skills, such as spelling, grammar, and syntax?
- Does my child have the ability to express appropriately complex thoughts when speaking or writing?
- Does my child demonstrate mastery of all age-appropriate math skills, such as mastery of addition and subtraction facts, multiplication tables, division rules, and so on?

These questions are a good starting place and may give you new insights into your child's academic situation.

## What's Going on at School

Parents will always need to monitor the situation at school and take responsibility for their child's learning. You should find out what your child should be learning at each grade level and match that against what your child actually learns.

The activity pages in *Learning Adventures* were developed using the standards developed by the professional teachers associations. As your child explores the activities in *Learning Adventures,* you might find that a particular concept hasn't been taught in school or hasn't yet been mastered by your child. This presents a great opportunity for both of you. Together you can learn something new.

## Encouraging Your Child to Learn at Home

This book is full of fun learning activities you can do with your child to build understanding of key concepts in language arts, math, and science. Most activities are designed for your child to do independently. But that doesn't mean that you can't work on them together, or invite your child to share the work with you. As you help your child learn, please bear in mind the following observations drawn from experience in our centers:

- Positive reinforcement is the key. Try to maintain a ratio of at least five positive remarks to every negative one.
- All praise must be genuine. Try praises such as: "That was a good try," "You got this part of it right," or "I'm proud of you for doing your best, even though it was hard."
- When a child gets stuck, giving the answer is often not the most efficient way to help. Ask open-ended questions, or rephrase the problem.
- Remember to be patient and supportive. Children need to learn that hard work pays off.

## There's More to Life Than Academic Learning

Most parents recognize that academic excellence is just one of the many things they would like to ensure for their children. At Score@Kaplan, we are committed to developing the whole child. These books are designed to emphasize academic skills and critical thinking, as well as provide an opportunity for positive reinforcement and encouragement from you, the parent.

We wish you a successful and rewarding experience as you and your child embark upon this learning adventure together.

Alan Tripp
General Manager
Score@Kaplan

Dear Kids,

Get your pencils sharpened, and put your game face on! You're about to begin a Learning Adventure. This book is filled with puzzles, games, riddles, and lots of other fun stuff. You can do them alone or with your family and friends. While you're at it, you'll exercise your brain.

If you get stuck on something, look for the Score coaches. Think of them as your personal brain trainers. You can also check your answers on pages 65–70, if you really have to.

We know you'll do a great job. That's why we have a special puzzle inside. After you do three or four pages, you'll see a puzzle piece. Cut it out, then glue it or tape it in place on page 64. When the puzzle is finished, you'll discover a hidden message from us.

So, pump up your mind muscles, and get ready to Score. You'll have a blast and boost your brain power at the same time.

Go for it!


Your Coaches at Score

NAME_____

# Get Into the Game!

**Can you fill in the gaps in Chris's story? Work with a friend. Without reading the story, one of you should ask the other for a word that fits the part of speech written under each blank line. Write in the words as you go. When you're done, read the story together. What you end up with may be wacky or wise, but it should be grammatically correct!**

My dad is a complete sports nut. Every single _____, he either
                                              noun

watches a game or plays one. He played football in high school, but in

college he _____ baseball. He wasn't a very
          verb/past tense

_____ player, Mom says, but what he lacked in talent he
     adjective

made up for in_____. These days, he keeps his baseball
                  noun

skills sharp by watching every game that comes on the

_____. He's also the _____ _____
     noun                          adjective          noun

of my school's Little League team. I don't play, myself. Dad

_____ me into trying out last year, but when I stepped up
 verb/past tense

to the _____ for my first at-bat, my _____
          noun                                    noun

got caught on the _____ _____. Before I
                     adjective          noun

knew it, I was flying _____ through the air. I landed hard
                         adverb

on my_____. Oh, _____! I was so
     noun/part of body        exclamation

embarrassed that I quit baseball, right then and there. Like my dad,

however, I'm a big, big fan. If a game's on_____ or TV,
                                              noun

I'm there!

> A *noun* is a person, place or thing. An *adjective* modifies a noun. A *verb* expresses an action. An *adverb* modifies a verb.

NAME _____

# The First Five

Who were the first athletes to win some of the most prestigious awards in sports? Look on the next page. Some of the letters in their names are given. The rest are in code. To break the code, solve the problem under each blank. Find the answer in the coded alphabet, and write the letter in the blank. When all the missing letters are filled in, you'll be able to name the pioneer champions!

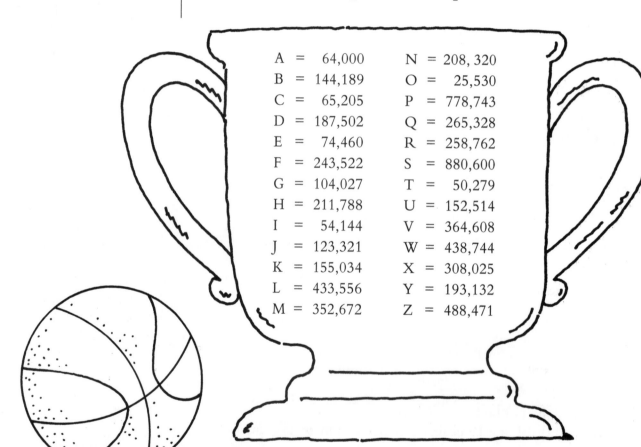

| A = 64,000 | N = 208,320 |
|---|---|
| B = 144,189 | O = 25,530 |
| C = 65,205 | P = 778,743 |
| D = 187,502 | Q = 265,328 |
| E = 74,460 | R = 258,762 |
| F = 243,522 | S = 880,600 |
| G = 104,027 | T = 50,279 |
| H = 211,788 | U = 152,514 |
| I = 54,144 | V = 364,608 |
| J = 123,321 | W = 438,744 |
| K = 155,034 | X = 308,025 |
| L = 433,556 | Y = 193,132 |
| M = 352,672 | Z = 488,471 |

**HOCKEY**

1. Who was the first winner of the Art Ross Trophy for leading scorer (1927)?

_____ **I** _____ **LC** _____ **O** _____
333 x 433    766 x 566    111 x 230    297 x 522

NAME_____

## COLLEGE FOOTBALL

**2.** Who was the first Heisman Trophy winner (1935)?

_____**A**_____
407 x 303   911 x 212

**BE** _____ _____**W**_____ **N**_____**ER**
427 x 606    992 x 210   125 x 512   539 x 193

## TENNIS

**3.** Who was the first winner of the women's singles championship at Wimbledon (1946)?

_____**A**_____**LI**_____**E**
987 x 789   687 x 222   210 x 992

**BE**_____ _____
137 x 367   893 x 547

## PRO BASKETBALL

**4.** Who was the first winner of the NBA Rookie of the Year award (1953)?

**D**_____**N**
230 x 111

_____**E**_____**N**_____**KE**
428 x 824   188 x 288   255 x 292

## MAJOR-LEAGUE BASEBALL

**5.** Who was the first winner of the Cy Young Award (1956)?

_____**ON**
413 x 454

**NE**_____ _____**OM**_____ _____
808 x 543   621 x 105   433 x 333   292 x 255

NAME _____

# Caught Cross-Checking!

Can you find and circle the names of all 26 teams in the National Hockey League hidden in this grid? (Here's a hint—they skate up, down, forward, backward, and diagonally.)

## Teams of the National Hockey League

- Avalanche (Colorado) • Blackhawks (Chicago) • Blues (St. Louis)
- Bruins (Boston) • Canadiens (Montreal) • Canucks (Vancouver)
- Capitals (Washington) • Devils (New Jersey) • Flames (Calgary)
- Flyers (Philadelphia) • Islanders (New York) • Jets (Winnipeg)
- Kings (Los Angeles) • Lightning (Tampa Bay) • Maple Leafs (Toronto)
- Mighty Ducks (Anaheim) • Oilers (Edmonton) • Panthers (Florida)
- Penguins (Pittsburgh) • Rangers (New York) • Red Wings (Detroit)
- Sabres (Buffalo) • Senators (Ottawa) • Sharks (San Jose)
- Stars (Dallas) • Whalers (Hartford)

A team name is a *proper noun*, so capitalize the first letter in each word. When you use the same words as *common nouns*, use lowercase letters.

```
S I F J M D A A D S N E I D A N A C
M A P L E L E A F S S Y S K A R S A
B A B V Y S H L S K C U N A C L R P
T L I R H E A V C W T S I S P D O I
B L U A E M R U A A T R U R R R T T
S Q R E E S D S R H W A R E E A A A
O K E S S Y M P S K O T B D D N N L
S P A N T H E R S C I S P N W G E S
L T P H X E H C N A L A V A I E S Q
J S G N I K W H A L E R S L N R O Y
L I G H T N I N G B R H J S G S V M
M S G P E N G U I N S R H I S T E J
```

NAME_____

# Hall of Fame Names

These pitchers all went by nicknames. All seven had skillful throwing arms—and impressively high win/loss percentages. Figure out the win/loss percentages. Then match each pitcher with his real name! One is done for you.

To get each pitcher's win/loss percentage, first add his wins and losses. Then divide the number of wins by the total, and round it off to the nearest hundredth.

| NICKNAME | WINS | LOSSES | PERCENTAGE | REAL NAME |
|---|---|---|---|---|
| Chief Bender | 212 | 128 | 62% | Charles Albert |
| Candy Cummings | 21 | 22 | _____ | _____ |
| Red Faber | 253 | 211 | _____ | _____ |
| Pud Galvin | 365 | 311 | _____ | _____ |
| Christy Mathewson | 372 | 188 | _____ | _____ |
| Kid Nichols | 360 | 202 | _____ | _____ |
| Dazzy Vance | 197 | 140 | _____ | _____ |

| WIN/LOSS PERCENTAGE | REAL NAME | WIN/LOSS PERCENTAGE | REAL NAME |
|---|---|---|---|
| 54% | James Francis | 62% | Charles Albert |
| 64% | Charles Arthur | 58% | Arthur C. |
| 66% | Christopher | 49% | William Arthur |
| 55% | Urban Clarence | | |

NAME _____

# The Mystery Marvel

Can you find out the mystery marvel's name and five facts about that impressive athlete? To find the mystery marvel, start at step number one and solve the number mystery. Then follow the directions. Can you keep yourself on the path to victory?

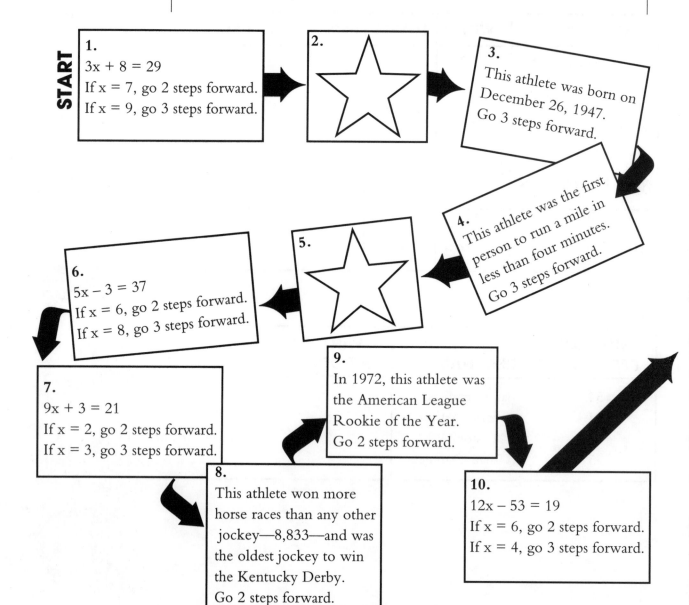

**START**

**1.**
$3x + 8 = 29$
If x = 7, go 2 steps forward.
If x = 9, go 3 steps forward.

**2.**

**3.**
This athlete was born on December 26, 1947.
Go 3 steps forward.

**4.**
This athlete was the first person to run a mile in less than four minutes.
Go 3 steps forward.

**5.**

**6.**
$5x - 3 = 37$
If x = 6, go 2 steps forward.
If x = 8, go 3 steps forward.

**7.**
$9x + 3 = 21$
If x = 2, go 2 steps forward.
If x = 3, go 3 steps forward.

**8.**
This athlete won more horse races than any other jockey—8,833—and was the oldest jockey to win the Kentucky Derby.
Go 2 steps forward.

**9.**
In 1972, this athlete was the American League Rookie of the Year.
Go 2 steps forward.

**10.**
$12x - 53 = 19$
If x = 6, go 2 steps forward.
If x = 4, go 3 steps forward.

**14.**
This athlete was a ten-time major-league baseball all-star. Go 2 steps forward.

**13.**
This athlete's 376 career home runs is the record for most homers by a catcher. Go ahead 1.

**15.**
$8x - 27 = 29$
If $x = 7$, go 2 steps forward.
If $x = 8$, go 3 steps forward.

**16.**
$18x + 7 = 61$
If $x = 6$, go 1 step forward.
If $x = 3$, go 2 steps forward.

**12.**
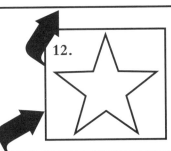

**17.**
$2x - 30 = 2$
If $x = 12$, go 2 steps forward.
If $x = 16$, go 3 steps forward.

**11.**
$4x + 19 = 35$
If $x = 5$, go 3 steps forward.
If $x = 4$, go 2 steps forward.

**18.**
Congratulations! You found the mystery marvel. At age 45, Carlton Fisk set the all-time major-league baseball record for games caught: 2,226.

**FINISH**

In each equation, the letter x is a *variable*—an unknown quantity. In $8y - 6 = 18$, y is 3. To get it, first add 6 (the opposite of -6) to both sides: $8y = 24$. Then divide both sides by 8: $1y = 3$.

Awesome! Now cut out the puzzle piece. Glue or tape it in place on page 64.

**Write the numbers of the steps that have the five facts about the mystery marvel. Then write the numbers of all the steps you landed on.**

_____

_____

_____

_____

_____

NAME _____

# Just the Facts, Folks!

The article on Battlin' Bruno's latest fight includes both facts and opinions. Can you tell one from the other? Circle each statement in dark type that's a fact. Underline each statement in dark type that's an opinion.

## BRUNO THE UNBEATABLE
### – by Flash Winston –

Last night, before his big match against Crusher Thomas, **Battlin' Bruno seemed unusually thoughtful.** Even though he was talking a mile a minute, flashing his giant smile for the TV cameras, when the cameras switched their glare to Thomas, **Bruno frowned and scratched his head.** "Uh-oh," said Pipsqueak Pomerantz, Bruno's manager. "When he does that, he's worried about something—and worrying's no good before a fight!" **Bruno had reason to worry. He and Thomas had fought five other bouts.** Bruno emerged the victor every time but, since their last fight, he had lost 25 pounds.

**In fact, facing off against Thomas, he looked downright fragile,** like a lone french fry next to a triple-decker burger. **The fight was scheduled for 12 rounds. The french fry didn't stand a chance.** They don't call him Battlin' Bruno for nothing, however. **At the very first gong, he came out swinging.** So did Crusher, of course. Crusher's size was no match for Bruno's speed. **With thrilling moves and fancy footwork, Battlin' escaped a pounding— Crusher never touched him.** By the third round, **Crusher Thomas looked crushed.**

*Facts* are true and can be proved. *Opinions* are what someone thinks or imagines.

**Around the House:** Look through a newspaper and cut out two or three paragraphs from a sports feature or other article. Circle statements that are facts. Underline statements that are opinions.

NAME_____

# What's News?

Lois Lake was covering an ice-skating competition for the local paper. But she came down with a bad cold and couldn't write the article. Help Lois by using her notes to write the story on another sheet of paper.

Place: Rayboro Arena
Sport: Ice-skating competition, men's and women's
Date: Saturday, March 8
Scheduled starting time: 1 P.M.

Lulu Pavlovich, Vicki Chin, Peter Madison, Benny Wayne skated singles.
L.P. favored to win women's, but . . .
Chin youngest competitor today.
Ouch! Madison fell attempting spin.
B.W. new men's champ.

Women's
Pavlovich: 8 — 8 — 7.5 — 9 — 8.5
final score: 8.2
Chin: 8 — 8 — 9 — 8.5 — 9
final score: 8.5
Men's
Madison: 6 — 6.5 — 7 — 5 — 7.5
final score: 6.4
Wayne: 10 — 9.5 — 9.5 — 10 — 9
final score: 9.6

V.C. only 14, never won—Lulu excellent but shaky landing cost her points—what's wrong with Pete? looks lazy (or hurt?)—Benny's a beaut, what a leap!

A news article should include facts that are accurate. It should also be interesting to read.

NAME

# Pitchers' Duel

Coach Zapper can take only three pitchers to the softball tournament, but she's got five great pitchers. Help her choose the best pitchers. Look at the charts below and on the next page. Then read the tips in the coach's corner. Then answer the question on page 11.

| Pitcher | Wins | Losses |
|---|---|---|
| S. FLAMETHROWER | 8 | 0 |
| R. ROCKETMEISTER | 6 | 1 |
| A. RAPIDAMENTE | 7 | 1 |
| M. NIMBLEFINGERS | 8 | 0 |
| J. WINGER | 7 | 0 |

After you answer the questions, try to throw this puzzle piece into place on page 64.

NAME_____

| Strikeouts | Walks given up | Home runs given up | Batters hit |
|:---:|:---:|:---:|:---:|
| 22 | 38 | 10 | 20 |
| 6 | 45 | 0 | 21 |
| 29 | 18 | 9 | 4 |
| 38 | 51 | 3 | 12 |
| 21 | 11 | 11 | 2 |

Try comparing each player's statistics, one category at a time. Rank them from best to worst. Then compare your lists, and choose the three that come out on top most often.

**Who should Coach Zapper take to the tournament? Give your reasons for each selection.**

1. _____

   _____

2. _____

   _____

3. _____

   _____

NAME _____

# Before They Were Stars

Can you match each NBA star below with the college he attended and the major subject he studied? To solve this puzzle, multiply the numbers below each player's name. When you multiply, you will get three lines of numbers to add together. The middle number will match the player's college on the list on the next page. The final sum will match the player's major subject. Round each final sum to the nearest hundredth.

**1. Michael Jordan**

    13.27
  X  2.83

    _____

    _____

    _____

    _____

Nearest hundredth: _____

**2. Shaquille O'Neal**

    57.72
  X  8.23

    _____

    _____

    _____

    _____

Nearest hundredth: _____

**3. Patrick Ewing**

    92.55
  X  4.13

    _____

    _____

    _____

    _____

Nearest hundredth: _____

**4. Scottie Pippen**

    86.54
  X  9.46

    _____

    _____

    _____

    _____

Nearest hundredth: _____

NAME_____

**Who?**

Multiply decimals
and round
decimal
quotients

**5.** Grant Hill

46.91

x  1.14

_____

_____

_____

_____

Nearest hundredth: _____

You multiply
decimals the same
way you divide whole
numbers. Remember
to use zeros to hold
your place.
Don't forget to count
over the right
number of places, to
put the decimal point
where it belongs.
Then round off the
number to the
nearest hundredth.

**Schools**

University of Central Arkansas—346,160
Georgetown University—92,550
Duke University—46,910
Louisiana State University—115,440
University of North Carolina—106,160

**Major**

History—53.48
Geography—37.56
Industrial Education—818.67
Fine Arts—382.23
Business—475.04

**Fill in the chart below.**

| PLAYER | COLLEGE | MAJOR |
|---|---|---|
| Michael Jordan | _____ | _____ |
| Shaquille O'Neal | _____ | _____ |
| Patrick Ewing | _____ | _____ |
| Scottie Pippen | _____ | _____ |
| Grant Hill | _____ | _____ |

NAME _____

# Megabuck Superstar

**Read about all-star athlete Dash Moneyman. If you were this player's agent, which contract would you recommend that he sign?**

When numbers get too huge to picture in your mind, they can be tough to compare—unless you remember to compare them by place.

Now, show me the puzzle! Put this piece in place on page 64!

Doodleburg Dribbles says, "Forget the rest, this is the best: Dash will be our star forward. We'll give him a seven-year contract: $9,880,000,000 to start, with an additional $24,100,000 in each of the six other years!"

Trish Mankovitz says, "We want Dash so badly, we'll guarantee him the top spot in our pitching rotation and give him a five-year deal worth $1,303,822,000 a year, plus a just-for-signing bonus of $6,100,000,000!"

Buck Fiddlehopper says, "We'll make Dash our number-one quarterback and give him a three-year contract worth $2,058,987,000 the first year, $5,456,221,000 the second year, and $7,500,326,000 the third!"

**Who should "Show-Me-the-Cash" Dash sign with?**

_____

**They're offering the most: a total of $ _____ !**

NAME _____

# What's Wrong?

A power shortage at the Wackyboro Sports Arena's scrambled the events calendar. Athletes from eleven different events showed up to play on the same day. To make matters worse, nothing else seemed to work right that day—not the equipment, not even gravity. How many things wrong can you find in this picture? Circle each one.

> Look beyond the obvious stuff. Consider what you know about such things as how gravity works or how much energy it might take to lift objects of various weights.

NAME _____

# Whodunit?

Look at this page and the next page. Solve the problem next to each person's name and the one next to each sport's name. Match the results to pair each person and the sport he influenced. Then fill in the blank in the paragraph on each sport with the correct name.

**WALTER CAMP:** $\frac{3}{5} \times \frac{2}{3} =$ _____

Walter Camp did not invent this game, but he modernized it. Camp played this sport from 1876 to 1882, while he was a student at Yale University. He organized and standardized the scoring system, as well as many of the plays and rules used in the version of this game played today.

**ALEXANDER CARTWRIGHT:** $\frac{1}{2} \times \frac{6}{7} =$ _____

Alexander Cartwright established many of the rules of this sport as it is played today. In 1845, in New York City, Cartwright organized a club devoted to the playing of this game. That year, and again in 1848 and 1854, he wrote down rules that soon were honored by all clubs and teams playing this sport.

**WILLIAM C. MORGAN:** $\frac{4}{5} \times \frac{1}{8} =$ _____

In 1895, William C. Morgan invented a game that he called *minonette*. The rules were simple so that it would be easy to learn and to play. By the next year, the name had been changed, as well as some of the rules and equipment. During World War I, U.S. troops serving overseas contributed to the rapid spread of this sport, now played all over the world.

**JAMES NAISMITH:** $\frac{8}{7} \times \frac{1}{4} =$ _____

James Naismith, a college physical-education teacher, invented this game in 1891. He started with simple equipment and 13 rules that he published in his school's newspaper. Before long, it was being played by professional teams throughout the U.S. and in Canada. Many of Naismith's original ideas are reflected in today's game.

To multiply fractions, first multiply the numerators. Then multiply the denominators. For example:

$$\frac{2}{3} \times \frac{3}{8} = \frac{6}{24}$$

$\frac{6}{24}$ can be reduced to $\frac{2}{8}$ and then to $\frac{1}{4}$.

NAME

**MAJOR WALTER C. WINGFIELD:** $\frac{4}{7} \times \frac{3}{2} =$ _____
The earliest version of this game was played during the Middle Ages.
The version played today is largely the invention of Major Walter C.
Wingfield, an Englishman. In 1873, he established rules for this game,
which he called *Sphairistiké*, a Greek word that means *ball playing*.
Among the key changes introduced by Wingfield was a ball that had
much more spring and resilience.

**BASEBALL:** $\frac{5}{7} \div \frac{5}{3} =$ _____
Today, baseball pitchers are allowed to throw overhanded, but in the
rules established by _____ , only underhanded pitching
was allowed.

**BASKETBALL:** $\frac{1}{3} \div \frac{7}{6} =$ _____
_____ was asked to come up with a game that
could be played indoors as easily as outdoors. Instead of today's rim,
net, and backboard, the first players made their shots in peach baskets
hung on a railing.

**FOOTBALL:** $\frac{1}{2} \div \frac{5}{4} =$ _____
In this sport, the number of points that a team gets for a field goal
(3 points) is different from the number earned by a touchdown
(6 points), conversion (1 point), or safety (2 points), thanks to rules
established by _____ .

**LAWN TENNIS:** $\frac{2}{7} \div \frac{1}{3} =$ _____
In the version of this sport established by _____ ,
the game was played on an hourglass-shaped court—widest at the
baselines and narrow in the middle, at the net.

**VOLLEYBALL:** $\frac{1}{3} \div \frac{10}{3} =$ _____
Today, this sport is played with six players per team. The original
version of the game, established by _____ ,
called for nine players per team, playing in three rows of three.

To divide fractions,
turn the division
symbol into a
multiplication
symbol and reverse
the numerator and
denominator of the
number that follows.
To solve $\frac{2}{3} \div \frac{4}{5}$,
do this:

$$\frac{2}{3} \div \frac{4}{5} = \frac{2}{3} \times \frac{5}{4} =$$

$$\frac{10}{12} = \frac{5}{6}$$

NAME

# Call the Shots!

Below are three different assignments and sets of items. Can you come up with a new game for each one? On another piece of paper, write a description of how your new game would be played. Include the object of the game and a list of rules. Be sure to give your new game a name.

Feel free to use each item more than once in a set.

Nice job! Now put this puzzle piece in the right spot on page 64.

1. Use or adapt these items for a game that would be played in winter on a snowy hillside. There should be two teams, each with a goal tender. Each team requires at least ten players.
   A kid's plastic beach bucket with handle and shovel
   A large plastic beach ball
   A large kitchen colander
   A pair of hiking boots

2. Use or adapt these items for a game that would be played in the shallow end of a swimming pool—indoors or out. There should be at least two players, but no more than eight.
   A tennis racket
   One plastic swimming fin/flipper
   A basketball
   A ping pong ball
   A volleyball
   An eye patch

3. Use or adapt these items for a game that would be played indoors, in a fairly small space. Use as few or as many players as you want, and have one referee.
   A tennis ball
   A soup ladle
   A large plastic garbage can
   A baseball catcher's mitt

**18**

**What?**

Learn how forces
acting on an
object change
its direction

NAME_____

# It's a Hit!

Look at the baseball below. Which part of the baseball in column A would you hit to make it go in each direction in column B? Write the letter of the correct answer on the line. The first one is done for you.

Try picturing the bat hitting the ball. Then imagine where the ball will go. Draw a picture if you need to.

| Column A | Column B |
|---|---|
| __h__ **1.** middle left | **a.** fly ball (up) over pitcher's head |
| _____ **2.** upper right | **b.** fly ball (up) to right field |
| _____ **3.** middle center | **c.** fly ball (up) to left field |
| _____ **4.** lower right | **d.** grounder (down) toward pitcher |
| _____ **5.** lower center | **e.** grounder (down) to right field |
| _____ **6.** upper center | **f.** grounder (down) to left field |
| _____ **7.** middle right | **g.** straight ahead, toward pitcher |
| _____ **8.** upper left | **h.** straight ahead; line drive to right field |
| _____ **9.** lower left | **i.** straight ahead; line drive to left field |

**Around the House:** It may be fun to try this same activity with a family member, but use a golf ball instead of a baseball.

NAME _____

# What's It Worth?

To win at darts, you have to hit the right spots that will add up to an exact score of 301 points, 501 points, 1,001 points, or 3,001 points. Look at the dart board. Then, follow the directions on the next page.

Remember, there's more than one way to earn each winning score.

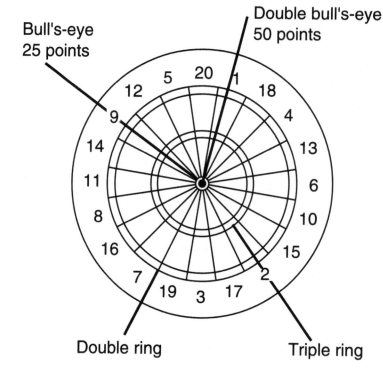

Bull's-eye
25 points

Double bull's-eye
50 points

Double ring

Triple ring

## DARTS SCORING GUIDE

- The board is divided into 20 equal-sized wedges.
- Each wedge is worth points, from 1 to 20 as labeled.
- The outer narrow ring is called the double ring. A dart that hits there is worth twice that wedge's points.
- The inner narrow ring is called the triple ring. A dart that hits there is worth three times that wedge's points.
- At the dart board's center is the bull's-eye. Striking the bull's-eye is worth 25 points. The small spot at its center, the double bull's-eye, is worth 50 points.

NAME_____

**How many different combinations can you find for each number of points? Write down the combinations. One is done for you.**

Strikes that will score 301 points:

1. <u>9, 7, Triple Ring 18 (54), 10, 20, bull's-eye (25), 4, 13, Double</u>
   <u>Ring 16 (32), 12, 5, Triple Ring 17 (51), 3, 6, double bull's-eye (50)</u>

2. _____

3. _____

Strikes that will score 501 points:

4. _____

5. _____

6. _____

Strikes that will score 1,001 points:

7. _____

8. _____

9. _____

Strikes that will score 3,001 points:

10. _____

11. _____

12. _____

**Check Yourself:** Double-check your answers to make sure each totals either 301, 501, 1,001, or 3,001 points.

**Around the House:** Challenge a family member to complete the activity, too. Did you arrive at the same answers?

Direct Hit! Now try your luck with this puzzle on page 64.

NAME _____

# Sneak Attack

Mr. Invisible is your football team's secret weapon. As a wide receiver, he's almost impossible to guard—but only when he's silent. Unfortunately, Mr. Invisible has a big mouth and always gives away his field position to the other team. To solve this problem, you have told him to communicate in International Morse code. To find out where the "I" man wants his pass, look up International Morse code in an encyclopedia. Use it to decode the letters. Then write the play on the line.

Remember to use International Morse code, not American Morse code.

1. •— — •• —•• • •—• •• — —• •••• —

   _____

2. ••• •••• — — — •—• — •—• •

   ••—• —

   _____

3. •—• — — — •—• —•—• —••• — — — — —

   —•••

   _____

4. •—•• •— — • •—• •— —••

   _____

5. •—• •—•• • •—• •—• •• —•—•

   —•—• • •—•

   _____

**Around the House:** Create codes for family and friends to decipher.

NAME_____

# Everybody Into the Pool!

It's your job to fill the pool with water. Use the diagram, the formula for volume, and the official pool regulations to figure out the pool's volume. Then follow the directions at the bottom of the page.

OFFICIAL POOL REGULATIONS
• The pool must be 164 ft. long.
• Each lane must be 8 ft. wide.
• The water must be 4 ft. deep.

◄———————— 164 ft. ————————►

64 ft.

To calculate the volume of a three-dimensional rectangle, use this formula: length x width x depth.

1. What is the volume of this swimming pool?_____

**Now calculate the volume of a proposed community pool.**

2. What would the volume be if the pool only had 6 lanes? _____

_____

3. What would the volume be if the pool had 10 lanes?_____

_____

4. Calculate the volume if the pool was only 160 ft. long. _____

_____

5. What if the pool had 8 lanes but each lane was 7 ft. wide? _____

_____

NAME _____

# Golf Club Caddie Quiz

Ever wonder why golfers—or their caddies—carry so many clubs around with them? Look at the chart. It shows the distance an average male golfer is likely to hit a golf ball using each type of club. Then follow the directions below.

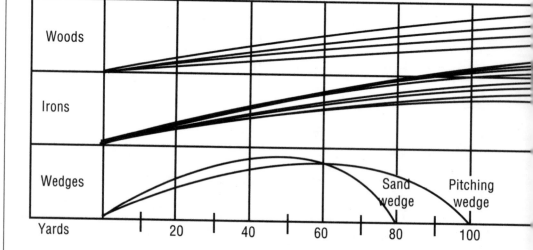

Hole in one! You know what to do now.

Circle which club you'll hand each golfer. The chart will tell you all you need to know. The first one is done for you.

1. Jaguar Woods is an average golfer. He is 140 yards away from the hole. You hand him a:
   Wood: 1, 2, 3, 4   Iron: 1, 2, 3, 4, 5, 6, 7, 8, 9
   Wedge: sand, pitching

2. Mr. Beemer, an average golfer, is 100 yards away from the next hole. You hand him a:
   Wood: 1, 2, 3, 4      Iron: 1, 2, 3, 4, 5, 6, 7, 8, 9
   Wedge: sand, pitching

3. Ms. Fairfax, whose shots tend to fall about 10 yards short of the average male's, is 200 yards away from her next hole. You hand her a:
   Wood: 1, 2, 3, 4      Iron: 1, 2, 3, 4, 5, 6, 7, 8, 9
   Wedge: sand, pitching

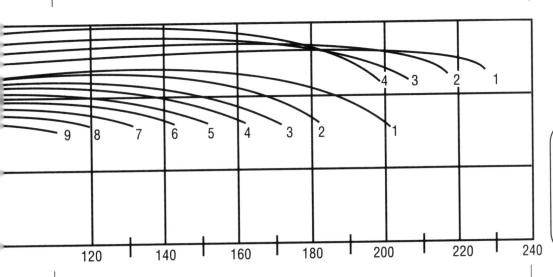

You may have to convert feet to yards before using the chart. Remember, 3 feet = 1 yard.

4. Mr. Hong's shots usually take his balls 20 yards farther than the average male's. When he finds himself 450 feet from his next hole, you give him a:

    Wood: 1, 2, 3, 4      Iron: 1, 2, 3, 4, 5, 6, 7, 8, 9

    Wedge: sand, pitching

5. Joey Jeenyus, the kid wonder, has a stroke as good as an average adult male's. But he doesn't want to make his golfing partner look bad, so he asks you for something that will make his shot fall about 10 yards shy of his next hole, which is 630 feet away. So you hand him a:

    Wood: 1, 2, 3, 4      Iron: 1, 2, 3, 4, 5, 6, 7, 8, 9

    Wedge: sand, pitching

6. Ms. Gomez is 600 feet from her final hole. Usually, she hits about 20 yards farther than the average male. Today, though, she is hitting about 45 feet farther than that. So you hand her a:

    Wood: 1, 2, 3, 4      Iron: 1, 2, 3, 4, 5, 6, 7, 8, 9

    Wedge: sand, pitching

NAME _____

# Law and Order

Look at the pictures below. Each row shows an athlete in action, but the pictures are out of order. Use what you know about gravity (not to mention momentum!) to number the pictures from 1 to 4 to show the correct order.

1.

a. _____    b. _____    c. _____    d. _____

2.

a. _____    b. _____    c. _____    d. _____

3.

a. _____    b. _____    c. _____    d. _____

**26**

NAME_____

# It's a Steal!

The time line below shows the all-time major league leaders in stolen bases and the seasons in which they made their records. It's up to you to figure out how many bases each player stole. First solve the problems inside the parentheses. Then add, subtract, multiply, or divide the results as asked. One is done for you.

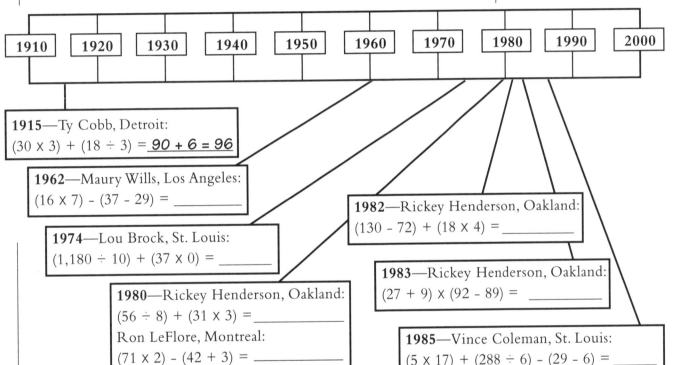

| 1910 | 1920 | 1930 | 1940 | 1950 | 1960 | 1970 | 1980 | 1990 | 2000 |

**1915**—Ty Cobb, Detroit:
(30 x 3) + (18 ÷ 3) = __90 + 6 = 96__

**1962**—Maury Wills, Los Angeles:
(16 x 7) - (37 - 29) = _____

**1974**—Lou Brock, St. Louis:
(1,180 ÷ 10) + (37 x 0) = _____

**1980**—Rickey Henderson, Oakland:
(56 ÷ 8) + (31 x 3) = _____
Ron LeFlore, Montreal:
(71 x 2) - (42 + 3) = _____

**1982**—Rickey Henderson, Oakland:
(130 - 72) + (18 x 4) = _____

**1983**—Rickey Henderson, Oakland:
(27 + 9) x (92 - 89) = _____

**1985**—Vince Coleman, St. Louis:
(5 x 17) + (288 ÷ 6) - (29 - 6) = _____

Now rank the top 3 base stealers, from most stolen bases on down. Fill in the chart below.

|   | Name | Year | Bases Stolen |
|---|------|------|--------------|
| 1. | _____ | _____ | _____ |
| 2. | _____ | _____ | _____ |
| 3. | _____ | _____ | _____ |

NAME _____

# Life in the Fast Lane

Since 1960—the year when women's 500-meter speed-skating became an Olympic event—eight different skaters have won the gold medal. Can you compare the times of these woman skaters? Look at the chart. Then answer the questions below.

| Women's Speed Skating, 500 Meters (1960-1994) | | | | | |
|---|---|---|---|---|---|
| Blair, Bonnie (U.S.A.) | 1994 | 0:39.3 | Henning, Anne (U.S.A.) | 1972 | 0:43.33 |
| Blair, Bonnie (U.S.A.) | 1992 | 0:40.33 | Rothenburger, Christa (East Germany) | 1984 | 0:41.02 |
| Blair, Bonnie (U.S.A.) | 1988 | 0:39.1 | Skoblikova, Lydia (U.S.S.R.) | 1964 | 0:45.0 |
| Enke, Karin (East Germany) | 1980 | 0:41.78 | Titova, Lyudmila (U.S.S.R.) | 1968 | 0:46.1 |
| Haase, Helga (Germany) | 1960 | 0:45.9 | Young, Sheila (U.S.A.) | 1976 | 0:42.76 |

Note: Times are in seconds and fractions of seconds.

1. Who is the fastest woman's 500-meter skater? (Remember, the smallest numbers show the fastest times.) _____

2. Which country holds the most gold medals in this event?

    _____

3. What is the difference between the fastest time and the slowest time? _____

4. How is the information organized on the chart?_____

    _____

NAME_____

Another way of seeing the same information is to put it into graph form. Here's how. Put the gold medalists in chronological order by writing each skater's last name on the line that matches the year she won the gold. Then plot her time on the graph. (The first one is done for you.) Then use your graph to answer the questions below.

Seven of the ten times include hundredths of a second. Round them off to the nearest tenth. After you have marked each skater's time with a dot, draw a line to connect the dots.

And don't forget to put this puzzle piece in place!

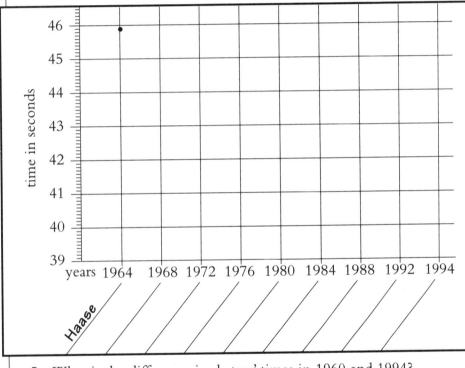

5. What is the difference in skaters' times in 1960 and 1994?

_____

6. How have the skaters' times changed from 1960 to 1994?

_____

7. How does the graph allow you to see this more easily than the chart? _____

8. When might you use a graph rather than a chart? _____

_____

NAME _____

# The Tour de Maze

Can you find your way through the bicycle course, from start to finish? First read the story below. Circle the preposition that best completes each sentence. Then use each preposition you circled to help you get through the maze on the next page.

## Pedals to the Medals

At the crack of the starter's pistol, all five bikers shot **(1) (a) over (b) through (c) into** the starting gate and headed **(2) (a) up (b) after (c) above** Dead Man's Hill. Randy Bates pulled **(3) (a) ahead (b) behind (c) across** of the other bikers almost right away, sailing easily **(4) (a) across (b) around (c) behind** the hairpin turns on the downhill side of the peak. Jake Timmons was in second place until he suffered a flat tire at Conway's Ridge and had to pull **(5) (a) into (b) over (c) under** to the side of the road. Raúl Montoya fared only a little better: just as he and Bates were sailing along neck and neck, Montoya's left foot slipped **(6) (a) onto (b) from (c) within** the pedal, causing him to lose his balance. By the time Montoya recovered, Bates was once again **(7) (a) of (b) on (c) in** firm command of first place. Then came Health-Hazard Curve. With Montoya, Calvin Richardson, and Zachary Soo all breathing down his neck, Bates took it a little too fast and almost went **(8) (a) after (b) into (c) out** of control. Weaving wildly, he barely avoided a crash. He fell **(9) (a) beside (b) over (c) behind,** to third place. As they entered the home stretch, Soo was in first place, Richardson in third, and a newly confident Montoya in second. Muscles screaming with the strain, Montoya poured it on. Somehow, he managed to push past the others and flew **(10) (a) under (b) across (c) over** the finish line, arms raised in triumph.

A *preposition* is a word that relates a noun or pronoun to another word in a sentence. Some common prepositions are *into, over, around,* and *through.*

Grades 5 & 6

NAME _____

# Scrambled Silly

The jokes on the opposite page are written in code—three different codes, in fact. The keys to all three codes appear below. It's up to you to figure out which code was used for each riddle or joke—then unscramble it. One code is used twice. Write the joke on the lines provided.

### THREE-STEP SWITCHEROO CODE

This code takes each letter in the alphabet and turns it into the letter three letters away. **A** becomes **D**, **K** becomes **N**, and so on.

| D | E | F | G | H | I | J | K | L | M | N | O | P | Q | R | S | T | U | V | W | X | Y | Z | A | B | C |
|---|---|---|---|---|---|---|---|---|---|---|---|---|---|---|---|---|---|---|---|---|---|---|---|---|---|
| A | B | C | D | E | F | G | H | I | J | K | L | M | N | O | P | Q | R | S | T | U | V | W | X | Y | Z |

### FLIP-FLOP CODE

This code simply reverses the alphabet: **A** becomes **Z**.

| A | B | C | D | E | F | G | H | I | J | K | L | M | N | O | P | Q | R | S | T | U | V | W | X | Y | Z |
|---|---|---|---|---|---|---|---|---|---|---|---|---|---|---|---|---|---|---|---|---|---|---|---|---|---|---|
| Z | Y | X | W | V | U | T | S | R | Q | P | O | N | M | L | K | J | I | H | G | F | E | D | C | B | A |

### ALPHABET-IN-A-BOX CODE

This code uses numbers instead of letters. Each letter is assigned two numbers: the first, its place in a row (across); the second, its place in a column (down). In this code, for instance, **C** is **13** and **X** is **54**. Since *y* and *z* have the same number, use the one that makes sense.

|   | 1 | 2 | 3 | 4 | 5 |
|---|---|---|---|---|---|
| 1 | A | B | C | D | E |
| 2 | F | G | H | I | J |
| 3 | K | L | M | N | O |
| 4 | P | Q | R | S | T |
| 5 | U | V | W | X | Y/Z |

When you've finished cracking the codes, put this puzzle piece in place on page 64.

1. **YVGGB:** SVB, WRW BLF SVZI ZYLFG GSV YZHVYZOO KOZBVI DSL QFHG TLG URIVW?
YLYYB: BVZS. GSVB URIVW SRN YVXZFHV SV DZH HL MRXV, SV DLFOWM'G VEVM XZGXS Z UOB!

_____

_____

2. **44 11 33 33 55:**    53 23 11 45    24 44    45 23 15    23 11 43
14 15 44 45    45 23 24 34 22
11 12 35 51 45    32 15 11 43 34 24 34 22    23 35 53    45 35
43 35 32 32 15 43 44 31 11 45 15?
**45 11 33 33 55:**    45 23 15    22 43 35 51 34 14!

_____

_____

3. **25 11 13 31:**    53 23 55    14 24 14    45 23 15    22 35 32 21 15
43    53 15 11 43    45 53 35
41 11 24 43 44    35 21    41 11 34 45 44?
**44 41 43 11 45:**    24 34    13 11 44 15    23 15    22 35 45    11
23 35 32 15    24 34    35 34 15.

_____

_____

4. **WLS:** LQ VSDLQ, WKH QDWLRQDO VSRUW LV
EXOOILJKWLQJ. LQ HQJODQG, LW'V FULFNHW.
**WRS:** LQ WKDW FDVH, L'G UDWKHU SODB LQ
HQJODQG.
**WLS:** ZKB?
**WRS:** LW'V HDVLHU WR ILJKW D FULFNHW!

_____

_____

NAME _____

# Bookin' It

When you look up a book in a card catalogue or on a computer, you will usually find a *Dewey classification number* which tells you where your book can be found. The five books below are missing their Dewey numbers. You can figure out their numbers by solving the math problems! Write the answer to each math problem in the second blank.

a. _____ *Sports Science for Young People* by George Barr

$26{,}274.27 \div 33 =$ (round to nearest whole number)_____

b. _____ *Volleyball: Play the Game* by George Bulman

$61{,}317.02 \div 77 =$ (round to nearest thousandth)_____

c. _____ *Strange and Amazing Football Stories* by Bill Gutman

$41{,}409.27 \div 52 =$ (round to nearest thousandth) _____

d. _____ *Famous Firsts in Sports* by John Jakes

$13{,}537.44 \div 17 =$ (round to nearest whole number)_____

e. _____ *Baseball Bloopers and Diamond Oddities* by Robert Obojski

$19{,}908.93 \div 25 =$ (round to nearest thousandth) _____

The books above are in alphabetical order by author's last name. In the library, they would be in numerical order first. Books with the same number would then go by the author's name. Next to each book title above, write a number from 1 to 5 showing the order in which they'd appear in the library.

NAME_____

# Alpine Percentages

Kitty Kowalski has been practicing hard to become a
championship-level Alpine skier. Find out how many gates
she cleared at her last race by calculating the percentage at
each gate. Then, round off your answer to the nearest whole
number. An even number means that Kitty cleared the gate.
An odd number means that she hit it.

To figure out a
percentage, first
change the percent to
a decimal. For
example, 25%
becomes 0.25. Then
multiply the decimal
by the number you
want the percent of.
To find 28% of 322,
multiply 0.28 by 322
(0.28 x 322 = 90.16).
Then round to the
nearest whole number
(90.16 becomes 90).

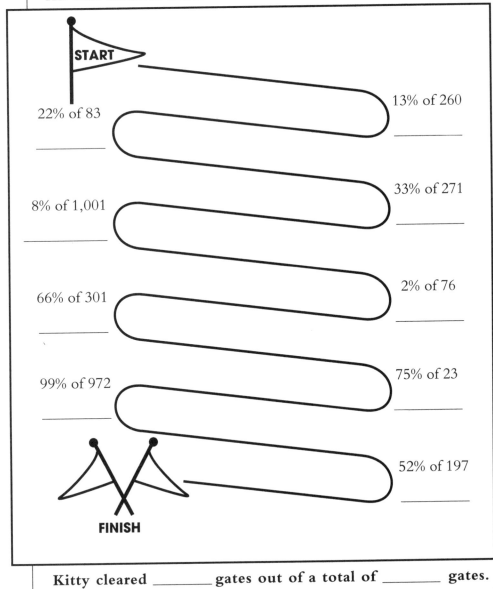

START

22% of 83
_____

8% of 1,001
_____

66% of 301
_____

99% of 972
_____

13% of 260
_____

33% of 271
_____

2% of 76
_____

75% of 23
_____

52% of 197
_____

FINISH

Kitty cleared _____ gates out of a total of _____ gates.

NAME _____

# Play Areas

Isabelle Wentworth has won awards in just about every sport there is. Her latest award is a plaque that declares her QUEEN OF 17,000 SQ. FT. That's how much space there is in a regulation playing area for one particular sport. On these two pages, you'll find sketches of regulation playing areas for 5 of the sports Isabelle plays. By calculating the area (square feet) of each one, you'll be able to figure out on which one Isabelle earned her latest award! Write each area in the blank.

Isabelle's latest award was for _____.

Don't forget to change yards to feet where necessary.

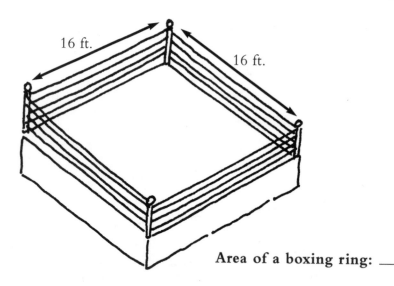

16 ft.

16 ft.

Area of a boxing ring: _____

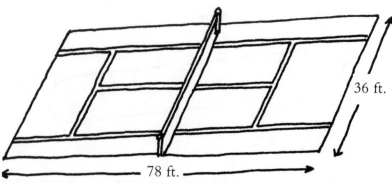

36 ft.

78 ft.

Area of a tennis court: _____

**36**

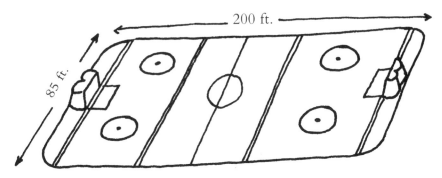

Area of a hockey ring: _____

You'll need to use the area formulas for two shapes: rectangles and squares. For rectangles, the formula is l x w (length times width). For squares, it's $s^2$ (length of a side squared = side x side).

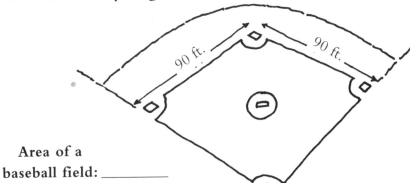

Area of a baseball field: _____

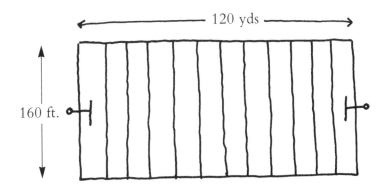

Area of a football field: _____

Isabelle doesn't like to admit it, but she's not so hot at one of these sports. Maybe 2,808 square feet is an area that doesn't agree with her. Which is Isabelle's weakest sport?

_____

NAME

# Where's the Game?

Mack and Emma compile information on each day's major
league baseball games. The trouble is, it's minutes from
deadline, and somebody has lost the list of where the day's
American League games were played. But they do know
where the home stadiums of the teams are. They also have
information about game times. "No problem," says Emma.
"We can use a time-zone map to figure out where the
games were played." Can you do the same?

## TIME ZONES

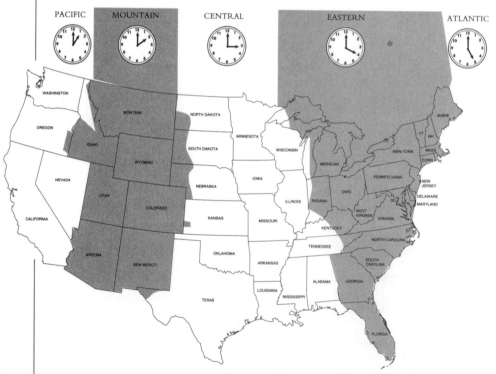

### AMERICAN LEAGUE TEAMS

| | | |
|---|---|---|
| Anaheim Angels | Detroit Tigers | Oakland Athletics |
| Baltimore Orioles | Kansas City Royals | Seattle Mariners |
| Boston Red Sox | Milwaukee Brewers | Texas Rangers |
| Chicago White Sox | Minnesota Twins | Toronto Blue Jays |
| Cleveland Indians | New York Yankees | |

NAME_____

**Read Mack and Emma's conversation as they sort out the mess. Use the time-zone map and the list of American League teams, fill in the blanks.**

### AMERICAN LEAGUE GAMES

**Mack:** The Yankees played the Brewers. The game started at 6:05 p.m.
**Emma:** Is that the time where we are or where they were playing?
**Mack:** The times are the same.

1.  The game was played in _____.

**Emma:** It says here the game between the Red Sox and the Twins started at 6:05 our time.
**Mack:** Yeah, but clocks said 7:05 where they were.

2.  The game was played in _____.

**Mack:** The first run in the Tigers–Mariners game was scored at 5:45 our time—a half hour into the game.
**Emma:** This says that the game started at 3:15 their time, so . . .

3.  The game was played in _____.

**Emma:** The Indians and Angels played two zones west of us, starting at 6:35 p.m. our time.

4.  The game was played in _____.

**Emma:** What a mess! The Blue Jays started at 2:10 their time. The Royals started at 1:10 their time and ours. The Rangers game started at 2:10 Eastern Time, but they weren't playing in that time zone.
**Mack:** That means the Athletics played one of those teams, and the other two played each other.

5.  The Athletics played the _____ in _____.

The other game was between the _____ and the

_____.

It was played in _____.

NAME _____

# Sky High

Here is a view from the blimp at a college football game. The blimp crew has already estimated that each circle represents approximately 100 fans. Without counting every single person, how many people would you estimate are at the game? Write your answer on the line below.

There are various estimating strategies that you can use. Try one of your own—or this one. Divide the crowd into sections of roughly equal size and shape. Figure out the number of people in one section, then multiply by the number of equal sections.

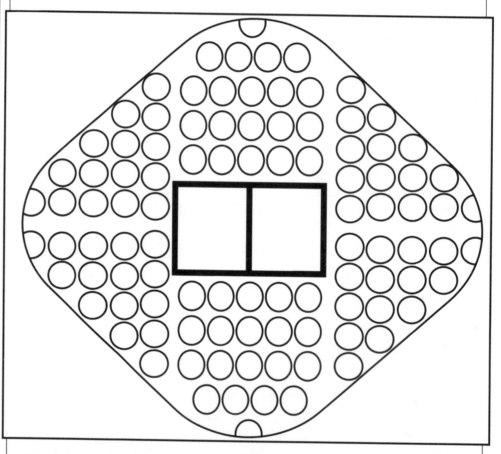

There are about _____ people at the game.

**Around the House:** Look through a magazine or newspaper for a picture containing a group of people too numerous to count. Ask a family member to estimate how many people are in the picture. Then you estimate the number of people. Are your numbers similar? What estimating strategy did you use?

NAME_____

# Screwy Scoreboard

Here is the scoreboard for a game between the Millville Mutts and the Tingtown Tomcats. Unfortunately, the scoreboard's computer malfunctioned and put letters where the number of runs should be. But there was a method to the computer's madness. Each letter was a variable in an equation. Once the computer operator figured out the equations, she knew the score. Can you do the same? Figure out the number of runs per inning as well as the totals. Solve each equation, and then fill in the chart at the bottom of the page.

In each equation, the letter is a *variable*—an unknown quantity. An equation's two sides are equal, which helps you figure out what the unknown is. In $8y - 6 = 18$, $y$ is 3. To get it, first add 6 (the opposite of -6) to both sides: $8y = 24$. Then divide both sides by 8: $1y = 3$.

| | RUNS | | | | | | | | | GAME TOTALS | | |
|---|---|---|---|---|---|---|---|---|---|---|---|---|
| INNING | 1 | 2 | 3 | 4 | 5 | 6 | 7 | 8 | 9 | R | H | E |
| Mutts | x | 0 | c | d | x | 0 | k | f | z | t | 47 | 12 |
| Tomcats | y | c | a | x | f | 0 | m | 0 | m | w | 48 | 15 |

1. $7a - 5 = 30$, so $a =$ ___**5**___

2. $28c + 6 = 34$, so $c =$ _____

3. $9d - 6 = 57$, so $d =$ _____

4. $13f - 8 = 44$, so $f =$ _____

5. $6k + 5 = 59$, so $k =$ _____

6. $4m + 37 = 45$, so $m =$ _____

7. $2t - 9 = 57$, so $t =$ _____

8. $5w - 71 = 54$, so $w =$ _____

9. $8x + 25 = 49$, so $x =$ _____

10. $11y - 23 = 65$, so $y =$ _____

11. $13z + 3 = 81$, so $z =$ _____

Here's the scoreboard again, ready for you to fill in as it *should* have been.

| | RUNS | | | | | | | | | GAME TOTALS | | |
|---|---|---|---|---|---|---|---|---|---|---|---|---|
| INNING | 1 | 2 | 3 | 4 | 5 | 6 | 7 | 8 | 9 | R | H | E |
| Mutts | | 0 | | | | 0 | | | | | 47 | 12 |
| Tomcats | | | | | | 0 | | 0 | | | 48 | 15 |

NAME _____

# Heavy Duty

In order to prove that he's the strongest man in the entire solar system, Mighty Mike will have to lift the same set of dumbbells on eight different planets. On Earth, they weigh 900 lbs. Since the force of gravity is different on each planet, he's going to need some help figuring out how much he'll have to lift on each planet. In the blank next to each planet, write how much the dumbbell would weigh on that planet. One is done for you.

| FORCE OF GRAVITY | | | |
|---|---|---|---|
| Mercury | 0.28 | Saturn | 1.2 |
| Venus | 0.85 | Uranus | 1.1 |
| Earth | 1.0 | Neptune | 1.4 |
| Mars | 0.38 | Jupiter | 2.6 |

To figure out how much the dumbbells will weigh on any planet, multiply the dumbbells' Earth weight by the planet's gravity force number. When multiplying decimals, be sure that your answer's decimal point is in the right place!

Mercury
Weight: __900 x 0.28 = 252__

Jupiter
Weight: _____

Venus
Weight: _____

Saturn
Weight: _____

Earth
Weight: _____

Uranus
Weight: _____

Mars
Weight: _____

Neptune
Weight: _____

**Around the House:** How much would *you* weigh on the moon and the various planets? How about your friends and relatives?

NAME_____

# Space Race

The race course in the Olympic marathon is 26 miles, 385 yards. At the 1996 Summer Games, Josia Thugwane of South Africa won the gold by completing the course in just 2:12:36 (2 hours, 12 minutes, and 36 seconds). If we could run at the speed of light, we'd need much longer race courses. Each athlete in the chart below is ready to run from a different planet. Assuming that they each run at the speed of light—186,000 miles per second—how many hours will it take each racer to reach the sun? Write your answers on the lines. One is done for you.

> To find the race time, divide each planet's distance by the speed of light. The answer will be in seconds. Divide seconds by 60 to get minutes, and minutes by 60 to get hours. (At each step, round off to the nearest whole number.)

| Athlete | Planet | Distance from the sun | Minutes or hours to reach the sun |
|---|---|---|---|
| 1. Mercurian | Mercury | 36,000,000 mi | 3 min. |
| 2. Venutian | Venus | 67,000,000 mi | |
| 3. Earthling | Earth | 93,000,000 mi | |
| 4. Martian | Mars | 142,000,000 mi | |
| 5. Jupiterian | Jupiter | 484,000,000 mi | |
| 6. Saturnian | Saturn | 888,000,000 mi | |
| 7. Uranian | Uranus | 1,800,000,000 mi | |
| 8. Neptunian | Neptune | 2,800,000,000 mi | |
| 9. Plutonian | Pluto | 3,700,000,000 mi | |

NAME _____

# Where in the World...?

This map shows some of the places where the earliest-known versions of some popular sports were played. Study the map and the map key. On the next page, write the sport that was played in each country and when it was played.

> Use the map key to figure out the where and when of each sport.

> When you've done traveling around the world, travel to page 64 and put this piece in place.

CANADA

UNITED STATES

| **Map Key** | | |
|---|---|---|
|  Badminton (pre-1800s) |  | Football (mid-1800s) |
|  Baseball (1600s) |  | Hockey (about 1855) |
|  Basketball (1891) |  | Soccer (400 B.C.) |
|  Bowling (5200 B.C.) |  | Surfing (before 1492) |
| Boxing (3000 B.C.) |  | Tennis (1100s or 1200s) |

**44**

NAME_____

EGYPT_____    FRANCE _____

CHINA _____    CANADA _____

INDIA _____    IRAQ _____

ENGLAND _____

UNITED STATES _____

_____

_____

NAME _____

# Play the Game

You're an alien who is studying Earthlings and knows
nothing about sports. Your job is to sort the following
recreational activities. You have noticed five main actions—
hitting, jumping, kicking, running, and throwing. Each of
the athletes on these two pages is involved in a different
sport, but some of the actions will overlap. Remember, you
don't know anything about rules or history or teams—all
you know is what you've seen the players do. On the lines,
write the letter of the action(s) you've seen each athlete
make most often. Then answer the questions on page 47.

**A.** HITTING
**B.** JUMPING
**C.** KICKING
**D.** RUNNING
**E.** THROWING

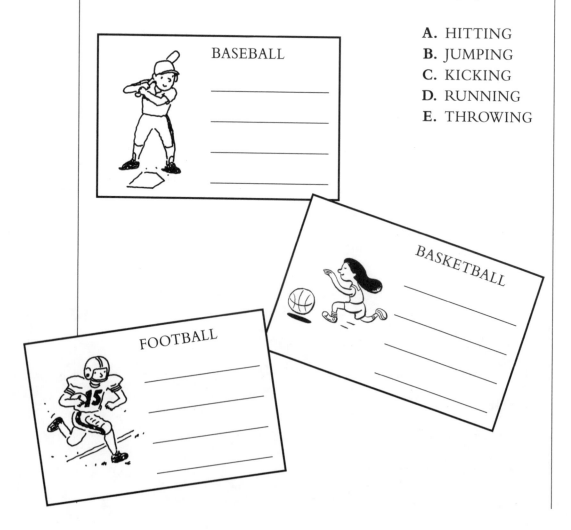

BASEBALL

BASKETBALL

FOOTBALL

NAME_____

FIELD HOCKEY _____
_____
_____
_____

SOCCER _____
_____
_____
_____

VOLLEYBALL _____
_____
_____

As you think of actions that fit each sport, think about what else these sports have in common.

1. Since you don't know the word "sports" yet, what might you call this group of activities? _____

2. Now that you've noted the patterns in these Earthlings' behavior, what do you make of them? Which would you group together? Why?_____

_____

_____

3. How are these sports similar? How are they different?

_____

_____

_____

NAME _____

# Bone Up on Safety Gear.

Here are some of the safety gear for three different sports. Next to each item, write the scientific name of the body part that it protects. If you don't know the scientific name for knee or wrist, the See-Through Kid on the next page will help you.

### IN-LINE SKATING

helmet: _____

wrist guard: _____

knee pad: _____

### ICE HOCKEY

helmet: _____

glove: _____

padded pants: _____

shin guard: _____

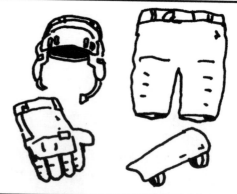

### FOOTBALL

shoulder pad: _____

arm guard: _____

rib pad: _____

hip pad: _____

knee pad: _____

# THE SEE-THROUGH KID

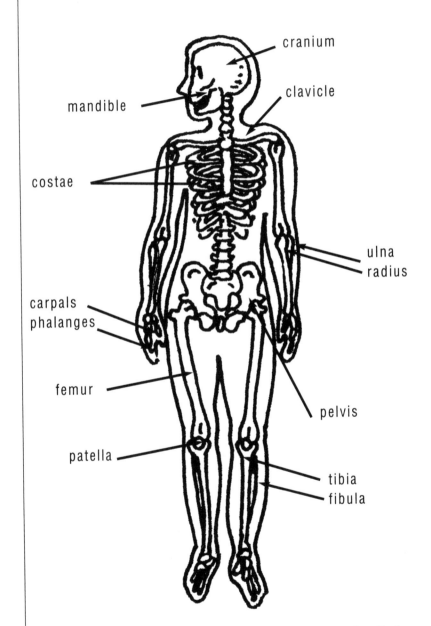

cranium

clavicle

mandible

costae

ulna
radius

carpals
phalanges

femur

pelvis

patella

tibia
fibula

Now that you know where all your bones fit in, see if you can figure out where this puzzle piece belongs.

**Around the House:** Does anyone in your family have a job that requires safety gear? If so, what part(s) of the body does the gear protect? What does it protect against?

NAME _____

# Montana's Numbers

This profile of Joe Montana has some numbers missing. After you solve the problems below, you'll know which number to plug into each blank. One is done for you.

### JOE MONTANA

**Born:** June 11, 1956 in New Eagle, Pennsylvania
**Height and weight:** 6 ft. 2 in.; 195 lbs.
**College:** University of Notre Dame
**College highlights:** Montana took Notre Dame to the national championship in 1977. In 1979, in his final college game, he took Notre Dame to a 35–43 victory—after they had been losing by a score of 32–12 with only [a]___5___ minutes left to play.
**NFL career:** 16 years, 1979-1994

- Super Bowl MVP awards: three—for Super Bowl XVI in 1982, Super Bowl XIX in 1985, and Super Bowl XXIV in 1990
- 1989: won his first NFL MVP award and hit his personal best for pass completions, [b]_____ percent
- Single-game records: #1 in yards gained—[c] _____yards (1989); #2 in touchdown passes—[d] _____ touchdowns (1990)
- All-time post-season records (23 games played): #1 in passing attempts—[e]_____ ; #1 in passing completions—[f] _____ ; #1 in yards gained—[g]_____; #3 in passing efficiency—[h] _____ percent completion
- All-time Super Bowl records: #1 in passing yards—68 percent; [i] _____ yards; #4 in passing efficiency—[j]_____ completions

a. 285 ÷ 57 = ___5___      f. 28.75 x 16 = _____

b. 23.4 x 3 = _____      g. (640.25 x 8) + 650 = _____

c. (58 x 6) + 9 = _____      h. 815.1 ÷ 13 = _____

d. 1,128 ÷ 188 = _____      i. 228.4 x 5 = _____

e. (2,310 ÷ 3) - 36 = _____      j. (588 ÷ 7) + 2.3 + 1.7 = _____

First, solve the problem inside the parentheses. Then do the rest of the problem. For instance, (98 ÷ 7) x 16 = 224. To get the answer, first divide 98 by 7 to get 14. Then multiply 14 by 16 to get 224.

NAME_____

# Is it Hot or Humid?

**Athletes must listen to weather reports and dress accordingly. They must pay attention to the *relative* humidity—how much water is in the air. Match each athlete's description with the weather report he or she heard. Check out the graph for clues. Then fill in each blank.**

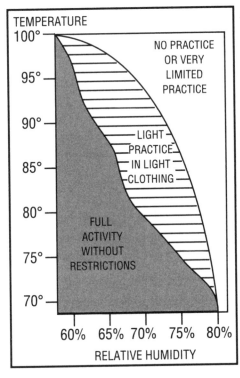

TEMPERATURE

100°

95°

90°

85°

80°

75°

70°

NO PRACTICE OR VERY LIMITED PRACTICE

LIGHT PRACTICE IN LIGHT CLOTHING

FULL ACTIVITY WITHOUT RESTRICTIONS

60%  65%  70%  75%  80%

RELATIVE HUMIDITY

**A.** I'm wearing shorts, a T-shirt, sandals, and a baseball hat. I am quite comfortable. I'm having fun playing horsehoes. I live in _____ .

**B.** I'm working hard to pedal up this hill. I'm wearing leggings, a long-sleeved T-shirt, bike gloves, a helmet, and socks and biking shoes. I live in

_____ .

**C.** I'm not running too fast. I'm dressed in shorts, a T-shirt, socks, and running shoes. I live in_____ .

The higher the humidity, the more water the air holds —and the less likely it is for an athlete's sweat to evaporate. When sweat evaporates, it cools our bodies. That keeps us from becoming dangerously overheated.

| **DES MOINES, IOWA** | **NASHVILLE, TENNESSEE** | **BUTTE, MONTANA** |
|---|---|---|
| A sunny day, with a relative humidity of 62% and temperatures in the low 70s. | Skies overcast all day, with temperatures rising to about 82°. The relative humidity will remain in the upper 60s. | Partly cloudy today, with a high in the low to mid 90s. Relative humidity 75%; chance of showers by evening. |

NAME _____

# The Good Word

Every sport, like many special jobs, tasks, or activities, has its own language. Here is a list of 30 sports-related terms. Do you know which terms go with which sports? Write the term on the line next to each sport. Some words may fit more than one sport.

alley • chainwheel • course • dribble • fairway • frame • gearshift • goalies • gutters • hat trick • heading • helmet • icing • irons • lanes • laps • motocross • par • passing • penalty • pins • puck • rink • slide tackling • spare • spokes • strike • throw-in • wedge • woods

**BIKING**
_____
_____
_____
_____
_____
_____

**BOWLING**
_____
_____
_____
_____
_____
_____

**GOLF**
_____
_____
_____
_____
_____

**ICE HOCKEY**
_____
_____
_____
_____
_____
_____

**SOCCER**
_____
_____
_____
_____
_____
_____

Good work, sports fans! Now, cut out the puzzle piece and find its spot on page 64.

**52**

NAME_____

# Why Does It Fly?

Ever wonder why golf balls have little pits all over them?
Those "pits"—called dimples—are what make a golf ball fly
far and high when someone gives it a good whack with a
golf club. The two diagrams below show why. Solving the
problems in the sentences will tell you a lot more. Write
your answer on the line above each problem.

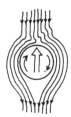 

When a golfer strikes a ball with a club, the two objects are in contact

for only_____ of a second. But a lot happens after that! A
$[\frac{1}{500} \times \frac{1}{5}]$

golf ball weighs_____ ounces. When hit, it spins backward
$[56.7 \div 35]$

as it flies through the air. If it had a smooth surface, the air pressure in

front of the ball would be higher than in the back, which would slow

its spin. It would travel only about _____ yards, then fall.
$[(20 \times 9) \div 6]$

But if the ball's surface is dimpled, the air pressure in front and in back

are almost the same. That means it can fly about _____
$[28.75 \times 8]$

yards before it falls. A golf ball spins at the dizzying rate of about

_____ complete turns a minute!
$[80,000 \div 16]$

**Around the House:** Check out some tools and other objects
used in your home. Do their shapes make them easier or more
effective to use? If so, can you figure out how or why?

NAME

# Muscle Up!

The names of ten key muscles are hidden in the puzzle grid below. They are the same muscles that are labeled on the drawing on the opposite page. Don't get scared off by those long names. You can find them! The names run up, down, forward, backward, and diagonally. Circle each muscle as you find it.

Bravo! Now that you've worked those muscles, how about some others? Can you add labels to any other muscles, telling their names and what they do? (*Hint*: Check out an encyclopedia.)

```
A  S  G  L  U  T  E  U  S  M  E  D  I  U  S
X  U  R  S  T  T  A  E  M  O  Y  Z  H  I  L
Y  E  B  S  L  A  C  I  R  B  M  U  L  U  D
L  L  J  E  S  P  E  C  I  R  D  A  U  Q  N
Z  O  A  D  S  L  E  E  P  L  I  J  R  P  H
T  S  S  D  I  O  T  L  E  D  E  L  T  M  A
P  P  U  L  L  Q  G  K  A  E  L  A  H  C  M
U  L  I  W  U  T  R  A  P  E  Z  I  U  S
S  Y  R  T  A  R  O  G  A  B  K  G  J  R  T
H  L  O  E  C  I  B  V  N  C  E  B  U  N  R
I  N  T  H  H  C  K  U  P  L  I  T  M  O  I
E  A  R  C  O  E  R  A  K  C  R  L  P  H  N
B  R  A  X  I  P  O  M  E  I  Q  W  I  L  G
O  R  S  T  E  S  L  P  C  U  L  U  R  S  S
B  Y  C  H  I  O  S  T  R  E  T  C  H  D  E
```

Here are eight other fitness-related words that are hidden in the grid. Can you find and circle them, too?

| | |
|---|---|
| EAT | RUN |
| JUMP | SLEEP |
| PULL | STRETCH |
| PUSH | TONE |

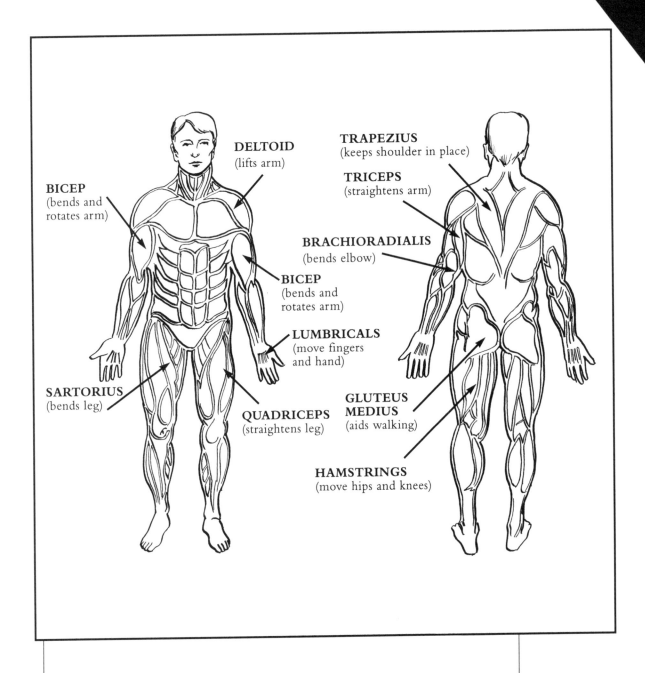

NAME _____

# Letter-Perfect Players

In 1996, Nancy Lieberman-Cline became only the eighth female player to be inducted into the Basketball Hall of Fame. Here are the names of the seven women who came before Lieberman-Cline and the years they were inducted into the Hall of Fame. Why can't you read them? That's because every letter in each name has been replaced by another—either by the letter that precedes it in the alphabet (with **Z** taking the place of **A**), or the letter just after it. (NANCY, for instance, would appear as MZMBX or as OBODZ.) Can you sort out the muddle? Write the names on the lines.

1992: KTBX GZQQHR and MDQZ VGHSD

_____

_____

1993: ZMM LDXDQR and KVMJBOB TFNFOPWB

_____

_____

1994: BZQNK AKZYDINVRJH

_____

1995: BOOF EPOPWBO and BGDQXK LHKKDQ

_____

_____

Did you know that the Basketball Hall of Fame is in TQSJOHGJFME, LZRRZBGTRDSSR? This time, the city's name is in one code, the state's name is in the other.

_____

Slam dunk! Now, take this piece and jam it in the right place!

GO!

56

NAME

# Energy to Burn

How many calories do you suppose an athlete doing each activity would burn in one minute? You can find out by solving the problems. First, solve each problem to get the number of calories. Then, using the word clue as a guide, draw a line connecting the calories to the correct sport.

Remember how to divide decimals? Do it the same way you divide whole numbers—just put the decimal in the same place as in your dividend, like this:

```
      20.7
  4 ) 82.8
      8
      2
      0
      28
      28
```

**a.** 3 ) 34.5
skimming a smooth surface

**Running cross-country**

**b.** 8 ) 112.0
making a real splash

**Skating**

**c.** 5 ) 35.5
raising a racket

**Playing football**

**d.** 6 ) 66.6
out for a spin

**Swimming
(at 55 yds. per minute)**

**e.** 7 ) 74.2
pounding up, down, and over

**Cycling
(at 13.1 mph)**

**f.** 2 ) 17.8
keeping the pigskin moving

**Playing tennis**

Which activity burns the most calories? _____

NAME _____

# Splash and Burn

A swimmer doing the breast stroke burns 11 calories per minute. How long would you have to do the breaststroke in order to burn off the calories in each of these meals? Write your answers on the lines.

Did you dive right in and figure them out? Nice! But if you need a hint— first add up the calories for each meal. Then divide the total by 11. (Round your answer off to the nearest whole number.)

### MEAL A

1 waffle: 215 cal
1 tsp. butter: 45 cal
6 tsp. syrup: 120 cal
1 glass (8 oz.)
orange juice: 110 cal

Total calories: _____
Swim time to burn calories:

_____

### MEAL B

1 hamburger & bun: 360 cal
2 tbsp. ketchup: 30 cal
1 malted milk-shake: 500 cal
1 frosted cupcake: 185 cal

Total calories: _____
Swim time to burn calories:

_____

### MEAL C

2 slices pizza: 135 cal per slice
1 can (12 oz.) cola: 150 cal
1 brownie: 140 cal

Total calories: _____
Swim time to burn calories:

_____

### MEAL D

1 hot dog & bun: 210 cal
2 tsp. spicy mustard: 10 cal
1 glass (8 oz.)
pink lemonade: 120 cal

Total calories: _____
Swim time to burn calories:

_____

**Around the House:** Check out the foods in your family's refrigerator and cupboards. How long would you have to swim the breast stroke to burn off a single-serving size of each? Choose one of the activities on p. 57. How long would you have to do it to burn off the same serving(s)?

# Drink Up!

Look at the cans below. These drinks are for athletes and other active people. But that doesn't mean you should just drink one without reading the label. Each was designed for a different purpose. When would you choose each? Read the questions that follow and write your answers on the lines.

These measurements commonly appear on nutrition labels: *g* stands for gram (about 0.035 of an ounce), *mg* for milligram (one thousandth of a gram), and *mcg* for microgram (one millionth of a gram).

### BEVERAGE A

**Nutrition Facts**
Serving Size: 1 can (12 fl. oz.)

Amount Per Serving
Calories 360 (90 cal from fat)

| | % Daily Value* |
|---|---|
| **Total Fat** 10 g | 15% |
| **Cholesterol** 10 m g | 3% |
| **Sodium** 250 mg | 10% |
| **Potassium** 500 mg | 14% |
| **Total Carbohydrate** 52 g | 17% |
| **Dietary Fiber** 1 g | 4% |
| **Sugars** 14 g | |
| **Protein** 0 g | |

*Percent Daily Values are based on a 2,000-calorie diet.

### BEVERAGE B

**Nutrition Facts**
Serving Size: 8 fl. oz.
Servings per container: 2

Amount Per Serving
Calories 50

| | % Daily Value* |
|---|---|
| **Total Fat** 0 g | 0% |
| **Sodium** 110 mg | 5% |
| **Potassium** 30 mg | 1% |
| **Total Carbohydrate** 14 g | 5% |
| **Sugars** 14 g | |
| **Protein** 0 g | |

*Percent Daily Values are based on a 2,000-calorie diet.

1. Which beverage would you choose to restore carbohydrates after a tough workout?_____

2. Which beverage would you choose if you couldn't have a lot of salt (sodium)?_____

3. If you had just eaten a fatty, cholesterol-rich meal, which drink should you avoid?_____

4. Which beverage would you choose if you were trying to lose weight by reducing your intake of fats and calories?_____

NAME _____

# Frank's Prank

Frank and Jen's mom left them two recipes for tasty post-practice treats. But Frank got home from the fields first and decided to play a prank on Jen by mixing up the ingredients. Can you help Jen unscramble the ingredients so that she doesn't get a bogus beverage? Write the ingredients correctly on the lines below. Then, on another piece of paper, write instructions for making Peanut Butter-Yogurt Delight and Icy Fruit Surprise.

Hint: each drink is made by mixing its ingredients in a blender until smooth.

Smooth moves! You're almost there. Put this puzzle piece in place on page 64.

1 cup of low-fat milk
1 cup of strawberries
1 or 2 tbsp. of peanut butter
2 tsp. of vanilla

3 or 4 ice cubes
1 banana
2 scoops of frozen yogurt
1 cup of low-fat milk

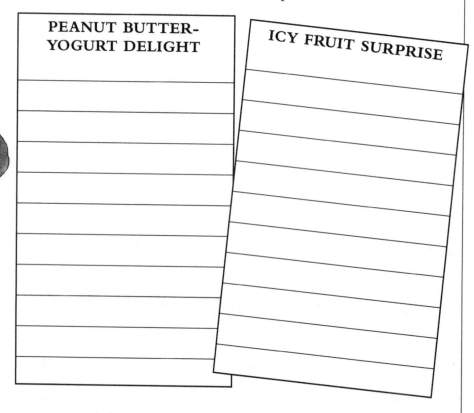

**PEANUT BUTTER-YOGURT DELIGHT**

**ICY FRUIT SURPRISE**

NAME_____

# Jake's Mistakes

Jake Smithers is in big trouble with his editor. The editor returned Jake's story all marked up with orders to fix his mistakes before the deadline. Can you help him out? On the blank line after each mistake, write (H) if he used a homonym or (A) if he used an antonym. Then write in the word he *should* have used. One is done for you.

In each case, Jake used a *homonym* or an *antonym* for the word he really meant to use. Remember what these are? *Homonyms* are words that sound the same, but are spelled differently and have different meanings, such as *sea* and *see*. *Antonyms* are words that have opposite meanings, such as *up* and *down*.

## JOLTIN' JOE (LOSES) _____ IT AGAIN!

NEW YORK, 1947—Today, baseball's big-wigs honored Joseph Paul DiMaggio, star player for the (Old) __New__ York Yankees, with the third Least _____ Valuable Player Award of his career. (The first two were in 1937 and 1941.) As modest as ever, DiMaggio (tolled) _____ this reporter, "It's an honor, of course. I'm just happy that I could help the teem _____."

Joe's fans are happy, too. "It's only (write) _____ that Joe should get the award," said Shirley Tyler, Bronx resident and deathlong _____ Yankee fan. "His bat helped the Bronx Bombers win the pennant *and* the (Whirled) _____ Series!" The Yanks beet _____ the Brooklyn Dodgers in for _____ out of seven World Series games.

No doubt about it: Joltin' Joe is a prize with a bat. He lost _____ the American League's batting championship in 1939 and 1940. Inn _____ 1947, he earned the home-run title by bashing 46 dingers. But his most impressive (feet) _____ so far may be the amazing hitting streak he had in 1941, when he got at least one safe hit in 56 games in a roe _____! If this reporter knows anything, he nose _____ this: Joseph Paul DiMaggio has already earned a first-class ticket (crooked) _____ to the Hall of Fame.

NAME _____

# A Razzle-Dazzle Finish

Remember how you started on page one of this book? Now that you're a pro, try it again. Remember not to peek at the story, just ask for whatever is under each blank. Once it's filled in, read the silly story aloud.

### A SOCCER SAGA

It was almost time for the final, deciding game in the junior high soccer league championships. Clem and Angie, proudly wearing their

_____ T-shirts, were on their way to the game. When
plural name of animal

they got to the field, they couldn't believe how many people were

already in the stands—_____ , at least. Suddenly, Clem grabbed
number

Angie's arm.

"Hey, _____ !" Clem said. "Look over there! Isn't that
silly nickname

_____ ? What's someone like that doing here?"
famous person's name

"You're a wacko, Clem," Angie said. "That's your grandma. Maybe

you need new _____ ."
plural noun

Just then, Coach Conway waved her arms and yelled, _____ ,
adverb

"Come on! The game starts in _____ minutes. I have
number

a few _____ words for you before we take the field."
adjective

Clem and Angie headed over to where the coach was

_____ ing with the rest of the soccer team. "Hey!" Angie said,
verb

"only _____ kids turned out to play today! This is gonna be a real
number

_____ game."
adjective

Congratulations, you did it! Now put in your final puzzle piece on page 64.

NAME_____

"I knew I should have stayed in_____ this morning,"
                                    place

Clem said.

"Listen up, you _____," Coach Conway said. "I know that
                plural noun

every time you go out on that field, you play_____. But
                                            adverb

today's game is more _____ than usual. If we win, we are the
                     adjective

champs. And Hank Banks, the TV reporter, is covering the game.
We're gonna be on TV. So let's go out there and win one for the

_____!"
   noun

The team played _____. The score went back and forth—
                adverb

first one team was ahead, then the other. The crowd screamed

_____ with every goal scored. Then, with only 10 seconds to
   adverb

go, Clem passed the ball to Angie, who gave it a _____ kick
                                                  adjective

that sent it spinning toward the goal. "Five!" shouted the crowd.
"Four! Three . . ." All eyes were on the ball. The other team's
goalie was leaping into the air, sure to block the shot. Just then a

_____ came out of nowhere and distracted the goalie.
   noun

Angie's shot went in! Victory!

Hank Banks and his camera crew came_____ ing over to
                                       verb

where Angie and Clem's teammates were _____ ing them on
                                          verb

their shoulders. "How does it feel to be a _____?" Banks
                                              noun

asked, sticking the microphone in their faces.

"Well, Hank, I'll tell you," Clem said_____. "There's just
                                          adverb

no _____ quite like it!"
      noun

"He's absolutely right!" Angie agreed.

THE END

A *noun* is a word that names a person, place, or thing— *woman, ballpark, football*. A *pronoun* takes the place of one or more nouns— *he, she, it*. An *adjective* describes a noun—*silly, happy, tall*. An *action* verb shows what the subject does or did —*hop, drive, fly*. An *adverb* is a word that describes how something is done— it tells more about a verb. Most adverbs end in *-ly—kindly, crazily, sadly*.

Grades 5 & 6

## 63

# Puzzle

Here's where you glue or paste the puzzle pieces you cut out. When you put them all in place, you'll see your secret message.

## 64

# Answers

## Page 1
Answers may vary.

## Pages 2-3
**1.** Bill Cook
**2.** Jay Bernwanger
**3.** Pauline Betz
**4.** Don Meineke
**5.** Don Newcombe

## Page 4

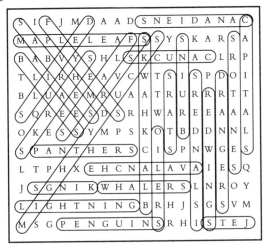

## Page 5
49%, William Arthur Cumming
55%, Urban Clarence Faber
54%, James Francis Galvin
67%, Christopher Mathewson
64%, Charles Arthur Nichols
58%, Arthur C. Vance
Best win/loss percentage (of these eight): Christy Mathewson

## Pages 6–7
The Mystery Marvel is Carlton Fisk. The facts in steps #3, 98, 13, 14, and 18 apply to him. The correct path to the Mystery Marvel includes steps #1, 3, 6, 9, 11, 13, 14, 16, and 18.

## Page 8
**Facts** (circled):
Bruno frowned and scratched his head • fought five other bouts • fight was scheduled for 12 rounds • At the very first gong, he came out swinging • Crusher never touched him
**Opinions** (underlined):
Bruno seemed unusually thoughtful • Bruno had reason to worry • he looked downright fragile • didn't stand a chance • With thrilling moves and fancy footwork, Battlin' escaped a pounding • Crusher Thomas looked crushed

## Page 9
Answers may vary.

## Page 10–11
Answers may vary.

## Page 12-13
1. Michael Jordan • University of North Carolina • Geography
2. Shaquille O'Neal • Louisiana State University • Business
3. Patrick Ewing • Georgetown University • Fine Arts
4. Scottie Pippen • University of Central Arkansas • Industrial Education
5. Grant Hill • Duke University • History

## Page 14
Dribbles' offer: $10,024,600,000 (9,880,000,000 + (24,100,000 × 6 = 144,600,000))
Markovitz's offer: $12,619,110,000 ((1,303,822,000 × 5 = 6,519,110,000) + 6,100,000,000)
Fiddlehopper's offer: $15,015,534,000 (2,058,987,000 + 5,456,221,000 + 7,500,326,000)
**Best offer:** Buck Fiddlehopper

## Page 15
**Things wrong:** baseball player using a hockey stick • pitcher's ball seems too heavy • barbells too heavy for how they're being used • male ice dancer has no way

of supporting his partner's weight—he's missing a blade • rider's momentum and position are wrong for getting over the hurdle • hockey player has a mix of soccer and hockey gear and is using an oar for a stick • goalie is in an impossible position and wearing flippers • no water/pool for diver to land in • boxer is trying to get a drink using a lacrosse stick, which will not hold water

## Pages 16–17

Walter Camp and football: $\frac{2}{5}$

Alexander Cartwright and baseball : $\frac{3}{7}$

William C. Morgan and volleyball: $\frac{1}{10}$

James Naismith and basketball: $\frac{2}{7}$

Major Walter C. Wingfield and lawn tennis: $\frac{6}{7}$

## Page 18
Answers may vary.

## Page 19
2. f
3. g
4. c
5. a
6. d
7. i
8. e
9. b

## Pages 20–21
Answers may vary.

## Page 22
1. wide right
2. short left
3. long bomb
4. lateral
5. flea flicker

## Page 23
1. The pool's length is 164 ft.
   The pool's width is 64 ft (8 lanes, each 8 ft wide: $8 \times 8 = 64$).
   The pool's depth is 4 ft.
   $164 \times 64 \times 4 = 41{,}984$ cubic feed (cu.ft.)
2. $164 \times 48 \times 4 = 31{,}488$ cu. ft.
3. $164 \times 80 \times 4 = 52{,}480$ cu. ft.
4. $160 \times 64 \times 4 = 40{,}960$ cu. ft.
5. $164 \times 56 \times 4 = 36{,}736$ cu. ft.

## Page 24–25
2. Mr. Beemer: pitching wedge
3. Ms. Fairfax: No. 3 wood
4. Mr. Hong: No. 7 iron
5. Joey Jeenyus: No. 4 wood
6. Ms. Gomez: No. 4 iron

## Page 26
1.  a. 4    b. 3    c. 1    d. 2
2.  a. 2    b. 3    c. 4    d. 1
3.  a. 1    b. 4    c. 2    d. 3

## Page 27
1915: $90 + 6 = 96$
1962: $112 - 8 = 104$
1974: $118 + 0 = 118$
1980: $7 + 93 = 100$ / $142 - 45 = 97$
1982: $58 + 72 = 130$
1983: $36 \times 3 = 108$
1985: $32 + 78 = 110$

1. Rickey Henderson, 1982, 130
2. Lou Brock, 1974, 118
3. Vince Coleman, 1985, 110

## Pages 28–29
1. Bonnie Blair
2. U.S.A.
3. 0:07.0
4. Alphabetically
5. 0:06.6

**6.** The general trend (with a couple of years) is that skaters' winning times have grown shorter over the years.

**7-8.** Answers may vary.

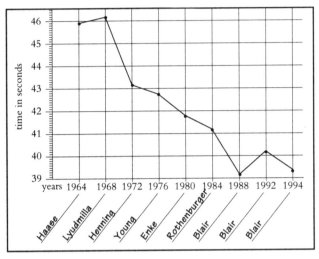

## Pages 30–31

| | |
|---|---|
| **(1)** through | **(6)** from |
| **(2)** up | **(7)** in |
| **(3)** ahead | **(8)** out |
| **(4)** around | **(9)** behind |
| **(5)** over | **(10)** across |

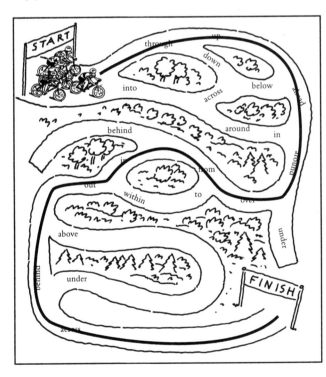

## Pages 32–33

1. flip-flop code
   **Betty:** Hey, did you hear about the baseball player who just got fired?
   **Bobby:** Yeah. They fired him because he was so nice, he wouldn't even catch a fly!
2. alphabet-in-a-box code
   **Sammy:** What is the hardest thing about learning how to roller skate?
   **Tammy:** The ground!
3. alphabet-in-a-box code
   **Jack:** Why did the golfer wear two pairs of pants?
   **Sprat:** In case he got a hole in one.
4. three-step switcheroo code
   **Tip:** In Spain, the national sport is bullfighting. In England, it's cricket.
   **Top:** In that case, I'd rather play in England.
   **Tip:** Why?
   **Top:** It's easier to fight a cricket!

## Page 34

**a.** 796
**b.** 796.325
**c.** 796.332
**d.** 796
**e.** 796.357

## Page 35

13% of 260 = 0.13 × 260 = 33.8 = 34 (cleared it)
22% of 83 = 0.22 × 83 = 18.26 = 18 (cleared it)
33% of 271 = 0.33 × 271 = 89.43 = 89 (hit it)
8% of 1,001 = 0.08 × 1,001 = 80.08 = 80 (cleared it)
2% of 76 = 0.02 × 76 = 1.52 = 2 (cleared it)
66% of 301 = 0.66 × 301 = 198.66 = 199 (hit it)
75% of 23 = 0.75 × 23 = 17.25 = 17 (hit it)
99% of 972 = 0.99 × 972 = 962.28 = 962 (cleared it)
52% of 197 = 0.52 × 197 = 102.44 = 102 (cleared it)
She cleared 6 gates out of a total of 9 gates.

## Pages 36–37

Boxing: 256 sq. ft. ($16^2 = 16 \times 16$)
Tennis: 2,808 sq. ft. (78 × 36)
Hockey: 17,000 sq. ft. (200 × 85)
Baseball: 8,100 sq. ft. ($90^2 = 90 \times 90$)
Football: 57,600 sq. ft. (120 yds = 360 ft; 360 × 160 = 57,600)
Isabelle Wentworth's latest award was for hockey.
Her weakest sport is tennis.

**Pages 38–39**

AMERICAN LEAGUE GAMES

1. Milwaukee
2. Boston
3. Seattle
4. Anaheim
5. The Athletics played the Blue Jays in Toronto; the Royals and Rangers played in Kansas City.

**Page 40**

There are about 9,700 people at the game.

**Page 41**

2. $c = 1$
3. $d = 7$
4. $f = 4$
5. $k = 9$
6. $m = 2$
7. $t = 33$
8. $w = 25$
9. $x = 3$
10. $y = 8$
11. $z = 6$

| INNING | 1 | 2 | 3 | 4 | 5 | 6 | 7 | 8 | 9 | R | H | E |
|---|---|---|---|---|---|---|---|---|---|---|---|---|
| Mutts | 3 | 0 | 1 | 7 | 3 | 0 | 9 | 4 | 6 | 33 | 47 | 12 |
| Tomcats | 8 | 1 | 5 | 3 | 4 | 0 | 2 | 0 | 2 | 25 | 48 | 15 |

RUNS / GAME TOTALS

**Pages 42**

Venus: 765 lbs ($900 \times 0.85 = 765$)
Earth: 900 lbs ($900 \times 1.0 = 900$)
Mars: 342 lbs ($900 \times 0.38 = 342$)
Jupiter: 2,340 lbs ($900 \times 2.6 = 2,340$)
Saturn: 1,080 lbs ($900 \times 1.2 = 1,080$)
Uranus: 990 lbs ($900 \times 1.1 = 990$)
Neptune: 1,260 ($900 \times 1.4 = 1,260$)

**Page 43**

1. 3 minutes
2. 6 minutes
3. 8 minutes
4. 13 minutes
5. 43 minutes
6. 80 minutes or 1 hour
7. 3 hours
8. 4 hours
9. 6 hours

**Pages 44–45**

Egypt—bowling, 5200 B.C
China—soccer, 400 B.C.
India—badminton, pre-1800s
Iraq—boxing, 3000 B.C
England—baseball, 1600s
France—tennis, 1100s or 1200s
Canada—hockey, about 1855
United States—football, mid-1800s, basketball, 1891, surfing, before 1492

**Pages 46–47**

Baseball: A, B, D, E
Football: A, B, C, D, E
Basketball: B, D, E
Field hockey: A, D
Soccer: A, B, C, D
Volleyball: A, B, D

1. Answers may vary.
2. Answers may vary.
3. Answers may vary.

**Pages 48–49**

**in-line skating:**
**helmet:** cranium
**wrist guard:** carpals
**knee pad:** patella

**ICE HOCKEY:**
**helmet:** cranium
**glove:** radius and ulna, carpals, phalanges
**padded pants:** pelvis, femur
**shin guard:** tibia, fibula

**FOOTBALL:**
**shoulder pad:** clavicle
**arm guard:** radius and ulna, carpals
**rib pad:** costae
**hip pad:** pelvis
**knee pad:** patella

## Page 50

**b.** 70.2 percent
**c.** 357 yards
**d.** 6 touchdowns
**e.** 734 attempts
**f.** 460 passing completions
**g.** 5,772 yards
**h.** 62.7 percent
**i.** 1,142 yards
**j.** 88 completions

## Page 51

Athlete A lives in Butte, Montana.
Athlete B lives in Des Moines, Iowa.
Athlete C lives in Nashville, Tennessee.

## Page 52

**biking:** chainwheel • course • gearshift • helmet • laps • motocross • spokes
**bowling:** alley • frame • gutters • lanes • pins • spare • strike
**golf:** course • fairway • irons • par • wedge • woods
**ice hockey:** goalies • hat trick • helmet • icing • passing • penalty • puck • rink
**soccer:** dribble • goalies • heading • passing • penalty • slide tackling • throw-in • hat trick

## Page 53

$\frac{1}{500} \times \frac{1}{5} = \frac{1}{2,500}$ of a second

$56.7 \div 35 = 1.62$ ounces

$(20 \times 9) \div 6 = 180 \div 6 = 30$ yards

$28.75 \times 8 = 230$ yards

$80,000 \div 16 = 5,000$ complete turns a minute

## Pages 54–55

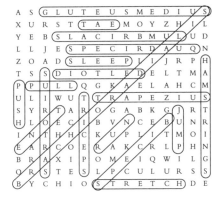

## Page 56

**1992:** Lucy Harris (letter before) and Nera White (letter before)
**1993:** Ann Meyers (letter before) and Juliana Semenova (letter after)
**1994:** Carol Blazejowski (letter before)
**1995:** Anne Donovan (letter after) and Cheryl Miller (letter before)
**Around the House answer:** Springfield (letter after), Massachusetts (letter before)

## Page 57

**a.** 11.5 calories per minute — skating (#2)
**b.** 14.0 calories per minute — swimming (#4)
**c.** 7.1 calories per minute — playing tennis (#6)
**d.** 11.1 calories per minute — cycling (#5)
**e.** 10.6 calories per minute — running cross-country (#1)
**f.** 8.9 calories per minute — playing football (#3)
The swimmer burns the most calories per minute.

## Page 58

**Meal A**
Total calories: 490
**Swim time to burn calories:** 45 minutes
($490 \div 11 = 44.5 = 45$)

**Meal B**
Total calories: 1,075
**Swim time to burn calories:** 98 minutes
(1 hour, 38 minutes)
($1,075 \div 11 = 97.7 = 98$)

**Meal C**
Total calories: 560
**Swim time to burn calories:** 51 minutes
($560 \div 11 = 50.9 = 51$)

**Meal D**
Total calories: 340
**Swim time to burn calories:** 31 minutes
($340 \div 11 = 30.9 = 31$)

## Page 59
1. Beverage A
2. Beverage B
3. Beverage A
4. Beverage B

## Page 60
Instructions for preparing each drink will vary as to details about preparation and steps to take. Accept reasonable responses with proper sequence. Sample answers include:

### Peanut Butter-Yogurt Delight
1 cup of low-fat milk
1 or 2 tbsp. of peanut butter
2 scoops frozen yogurt

First, place the milk, peanut butter, and frozen yogurt in a blender. Then, blend until smooth.

### Icy-Fruit Surprise
1 cup of low-fat milk
1 banana
1 cup of strawberries
2 tsp. of vanilla
3 or 4 ice cubes

First, peel the banana and cut the tops off of the strawberries. Next, place the milk, banana, strawberries, vanilla, and ice cubes in a blender. Then, blend until smooth.

## Page 61
**loses:** (A) wins
**Least:** (A) Most
**tolled:** (H) told
**teem:** (H) team
**write:** (H) right
**deathlong:** (A) lifelong
**Whirled:** (H) World (World Series)
**beet:** (H) beat
**for:** (H) four
**lost:** (A) won
**Inn:** (H) In
**feet:** (H) feat
**roe:** (H) row
**nose:** (H) knows
**crooked:** (A) straight

## Pages 62–63
Answers may vary but should include the correct part of speech.

# How Do You Foster Your Child's Interest in Learning?

In preparing this series, we surveyed scores of parents on this key question. Here are some of the best suggestions:

- Take weekly trips to the library to take out books, and attend special library events.

- Have lots of books around the house, especially on topics of specific interest to children.

- Read out loud nightly.

- Take turns reading to each other.

- Subscribe to age-appropriate magazines.

- Point out articles of interest in the newspaper or a magazine.

- Tell each other stories.

- Encourage children to write journal entries and short stories.

- Ask them to write letters and make cards for special occasions.

- Discuss all the things you do together.

- Limit TV time.

- Watch selected programs on TV together, like learning/educational channels.

- Provide project workbooks purchased at teacher supply stores.

- Supply lots of arts and crafts materials and encourage children to be creative.

- Encourage children to express themselves in a variety of ways.

- Take science and nature walks.

- Teach children to play challenging games such as chess.

- Provide educational board games.

- Supply lots of educational and recreational computer games.

- Discuss what children are learning and doing on a daily basis.

- Invite classmates and other friends over to your house for team homework assignments.

- Keep the learning experiences fun for children.

- Help children with their homework and class assignments.

- Take trips to museums and museum classes.

- Visits cities of historical interest.

- Takes trips to the ocean and other fun outdoor locations (fishing at lakes, mountain hikes).

- Visit the aquarium and zoo.

- Cook, bake, and measure ingredients.

- Encourage children to participate in sports.

- Listen to music, attend concerts, and encourage children to take music lessons.

- Be positive about books, trips, and other daily experiences.

- Take family walks.

- Let children be part of the family decision-making process.

- Sit down together to eat and talk.

- Give a lot of praise and positive reinforcement for your child's efforts.

- Review child's homework that has been returned by the teacher.

- Encourage children to use resources such as the dictionary, encyclopedia, thesaurus, and atlas.

- Plant a vegetable garden outdoors or in pots in your kitchen.

- Make each child in your family feel he or she is special.

- Don't allow children to give up, especially when it comes to learning and dealing with challenges.

- Instill a love of language; it will expose your child to a richer thought bank.

- Tell your children stories that share, not necessarily teach a lesson.

- Communicate your personal processes with your children.

- Don't talk about what your child did not do. Put more interest on what your child did do. Accept where your child is at, and praise his or her efforts.

- Express an interest in children's activities and schoolwork.

- Limit TV viewing time at home and foster good viewing habits.

- Work on enlarging children's vocabulary.

- Emphasize learning accomplishments, no matter how small.

- Go at their own pace; People learn at different rates.

- Challenge children to take risks.

- Encourage them to do their best, not be the best.